SOUL DEEP IN HORSES

Memoir of an Equestrian Vagabond

MERRI MELDE

• The Equestrian Vagabond •

For my Family, and for The Horses, of course

Published by
The Equestrian Vagabond
Merri Melde
P.O. Box 5
Murphy, Idaho 83650

www.TheEquestrianVagabond.com

Manufactured in the United States

ISBN: Soft cover 978.0.9913460.6.6
eBook 978.0.9913460.9.7

Table of Contents

FOREWORD

Webster's dictionary defines a free spirit as "someone who lives without regard to or what convention dictates or what others expect." I could have stated it in two words . . . Merri Melde.

Merri Melde's provocative prose puts the reader into peripatetic shoes as no other writer has ever done for me. You are viewing the world through her eyes rather than your own; you are walking in her shoes, not your own; you are sitting in her saddle, not riding beside her. Her words are not fancy nor meant to impress. They are used to masterfully tell stories.

The adventuress Merri shares with you the same enthusiasm she has felt as she embarked upon each new life journey, whether it be backpacking around the world, building trails for the Forest Service, driving a horse carriage, surveying spotted owls, working as a theater sound engineer or as a photojournalist, or carrying out her present role of conditioning and competing on endurance horses—jobs as varied as her interests.

In her short story *Traveler Tales,* you take every frozen tortuous step with Merri as she ascends to nearly 18,000 feet in the Himalayas. You gasp for air as she is thrown from her raft into the turbulent rapids of the great Zambezi River. You laugh empathetically at her frustration when trying to mail a package in India. Your feet ache as she backpacks through Europe, southern Africa, and Southeast Asia.

For ten years she groomed and shared the vicissitudes of the racehorses moving emotionally through her life, and we feel her close kinships with them, in her short story *Racehorse Tales.*

We accompany her in the saddle as her paths lead her to faraway Egypt, or as she leads a string of packhorses in the mountains.

This is when the real truth comes out; Merri's soul is revealed. Her life is horses . . . the good and not so good; but all stir her passion, and many instill a deep abiding love. Through her words, photography, and art, her life is simply horses.

Merri's acclaimed magazine cover photos and articles would fill several large scrapbooks, each tale broadening the horse world to those lucky enough to turn the pages. Combined with text, her candid action shots bring us her favorite animal at play—rolling in the mud, running in a winter storm, and stirring our souls with the faraway look of eagles. Her clever horse cartoons hilariously tell stories from the horse's viewpoint.

They frequently feature her horse, Stormy, the horse she never lets the reader forget is The Most Beautiful Horse On The Planet. We will forgive her momentary lapse, as most horse owners know full well the horse matching that description resides in their corral.

Referring to herself as The Equestrian Vagabond, an apt title earned and respected by her fans, Merri's photographs and her stories vicariously bring to us adventures that enrich our lives. She delights in her daily existence, whether it's with the animals she loves best riding in Malaysia, Ireland, or her own Idaho desert back yard, where her horse leaves hoof prints along the Snake River bank.

Merri is enthralled with the equine world (and Stormy, in particular). Her inquiring mind won't rest until it knows what is beyond the next bend in the road, what is on the other side of that hill, where that desolate canyon in Owyhee country leads, or why the hawks are circling above, all seen best, of course, from the saddle.

When you turn the last page of *Soul Deep in Horses: Memoir of an Equestrian Vagabond*, you will not close the cover and put it by your chair. You will flip back to page one to walk in the shoes and sit in the saddle of a free spirit again.

JULIE SUHR
Hall of Fame Endurance Rider
Scotts Valley, California

PROLOGUE

It's always been horses.

The feel of gentleness and power, the sense of willingness and innate wildness, the scent of earth and life and perfection, and oh, just the sight of them that steals your breath away. Those rippling muscles, the long legs, the flowing mane you can twist your fingers around and bury your head in, and the eyes—the expressive eyes that don't lie and can reach in and ensnare your heart.

It wasn't a conscious choice, this life with horses. I was already born with their hoof prints on my heart, and I knew no other way. By the time I first sat on a horse at around age eleven after much persistence (or maybe more accurately, annoyance to my parents), horses had already worked down into my bones and settled in my soul, and it was far too late for anybody to try to transfuse them out, if even they'd had the foresight.

For a while early on, when I became aware of the passion, I was convinced I must have been secretly adopted, because no one else in my family had (or has) ever been so obsessed with horses.

Am I a throwback to some ancestor who grew up knowing horses like the back of her hand, galloping free, saddle-less and bridle-less across the mountains, merging as one with my beast, speaking, thinking, knowing, being Horse?

I didn't set out to follow my dreams. I simply followed the horses, unquestioning, trusting, wherever their trails led: to the fields around my childhood home, to a working ranch, to the racetrack, to the mountains and deserts, to foreign countries. Horses have turned my comprehension of life upside down, wrung me inside out, made me laugh, made me cry, with despondency and joy. They have enlightened me; they have perplexed and exasperated and defeated me. They've thrilled me, and they've scared and disappointed me;

they've hurt me, broken me, drug me to the abyss of pain, and almost killed me. They've put me on top of the world.

And still I willingly run down that trail alongside them, dancing in their hoof prints, discovering the next unforeseen dream and finding the next treasure, reverently and deferentially clutching the next gift they unselfishly share with me. The desire to ride a trusted horse is almost a physical ache, a fathomless void to fill, something I am helplessly bound to pursuing the rest of my life.

I have been lucky. I gratefully chase horses in the day and I dream of them in the night, even now, after all these years.

Chapter 1—Washington State

SHATTERED

Thundering hoof beats shook the core of my soul.

The fluttering of windswept mane, the rush of power, the thrill of flight, fast and wild—galloping on a horse had long been my dream.

Only here the drumming thunder pounded the death knell. The ground streaked beneath my feet. Scenery whirled by in an unrecognizable blur. Whipping mane slashed me in the face. Wind roared in my ears, ridiculing me: *COWARD!*

I was on a runaway horse, and I was going to die.

Exhaustion shouldered aside panic, creeping viciously through my muscles, inexorably, down my arms, into my fingertips, squeezing down my thighs, into my calves, slowly rendering me incapable of staying centered and upright on the back of this out-of-control horse.

An overwhelming sense of sheer helplessness engulfed me as no wave of adrenaline ever could. An urge to weep strangled me. The wind ripped stinging tears from my eyes.

COWARD!

I just wanted it to stop. Letting go—sliding out of the saddle was a seductive proposition.

The reins—my lifeline—began slipping from my fingers. My vision swirled; my will sank into a downward spiral of defeat. My body began to sway in the saddle. I longed for the ground—the ground that rushed beneath my horse's churning hooves and threatened to shatter me to bits if I slammed into it at this speed.

I had thought living my dream was supposed to be thrilling. Fulfilling. Living my dream wasn't supposed to end like this: in pieces.

I didn't want to win the Kentucky Derby. I didn't even want to ride in a horse race. I wanted to gallop horses. It was the ultimate dream job, exercising horses on the racetrack.

No idea where it came from, but I'd grown up a starry-eyed child infatuated with horses, the only one in my family with the affliction. Probably the fact that I never did get a horse as I was growing up only fanned the flames of horse obsession. Maybe if my parents *had* given me a horse, equines would have been a passing phase. But they didn't feel the need to add a huge four-legged creature to our household, and regardless of the reason, I'm as obsessed now, forty years later, as I was then.

I spent the last two years of high school, on summers and weekends, working on the legendary King Ranch in south Texas, after I bugged them to no end for a job. I think they finally gave me one so I'd leave them alone. I started out helping in the office, while always keeping my attention focused out the windows, on the royally bred ranch Quarter Horses I could see in the distance: Mr. San Peppy and Peppy San Badger (known as Little Peppy).

I met Buster Welch, who consulted, trained for, and managed the King Ranch about the time that he was on his way to becoming famous. He was so tickled with my enthusiasm and my name, "Merry Melody," that he said he was going to name a colt after me: Peppy's Merry Melody. I don't think he ever did, but that's how I've always remembered Buster Welch.

After spending a month or so in the office, I'd wormed my way into working with the broodmare operation, feeding and learning to handle the Quarter Horse mares and foals. Occasionally I'd sneak out on a ranch horse for a ride, as if I knew what I was doing.

Jackrabbit, one of those cow ponies, ran off with me once in a big pasture, but I wasn't scared; I simply steered him straight toward a barbed wire fence. I knew he'd stop. It was a game of chicken—and I knew I'd win, and I did. Jackrabbit skidded to a 45-degree stop-turn right at the fence. I stayed in the saddle. We continued on our ride. The possibility of flying off into the barbed wire never occurred to me. I was that sure of my seat.

I thought I was a pretty darn good rider, those days on the working horses on the King Ranch. And maybe I was, back then as a kid. At that age, you don't know yet how much you don't know. Ignorance makes you fearless.

But somewhere along the way, I grew up and realized I didn't *really* know how to ride that well, and that horses were big and very powerful when they wanted to be; and I discovered I was mortal and my bones were indeed breakable.

Four years of college in Texas kept me away from horses, though I started studying Animal Science. That became unappealing when courses like "Meats," where I'd be carving up my very own cow carcasses, appeared on my curriculum. There were a lot of dip-chewing cowboys in the classes who talked with those slow drawls, and that atmosphere didn't quite appeal to me then, either.

From watching thrilling Thoroughbred races and great horses on television, and after visiting a racetrack one time, there had always been a dream of riding racehorses floating around all fluffy-like in my head, and I didn't quite picture cowboys, snuff, and "Soil Sciences" or "Meats" getting me there. I switched to Biomedical Science as a major, because that was at least more interesting, though I had no desire to continue on to medical or veterinary school.

"That's a great degree you have!" people always said, after I graduated with honors and a Bachelor's degree. "You'll be able to go far with that!" (All these years later, people still hold out hope for me and that still-unused degree.)

I went as far as the racetrack. I took my degree and my Horse Galloping Fantasies that were still nipping at me, and I moved to Seattle. My new neighbors just happened to own racehorses. They took me on the backstretch of Longacres racetrack one day, and I fell in love. I wanted to work at the track because this was where I knew I was meant to be.

The friends set me up with a good trainer, Ben Harris, and I started work the next year as a groom, with five beautiful Thoroughbreds in my charge. I even won two races with them that year. I'm sure the wins were easily attributable to my excellent care.

It was hard work, seven days a week, starting at 4:30 a.m. And I was *not* a morning person. The hours could be long—six to eight hours in the morning, and up to six hours at night, if I had a horse or two running in the evening races. Sometimes I got home at 11:30 at night, and I was back in the barn at 4:30 the next morning. We worked in the heat, the rain, the snow, and the bitter cold. I never had a day off. I didn't want a day off. My horses would have missed me if I'd taken a day off. I woke up late only once in those six years, and arrived twenty minutes late at the barn where I was immediately chewed out. Not by my boss, but by Chalk Box, who was used to getting out of her stall promptly at 4:35, every morning of every week of every month of the season.

Mornings were busy: unbandaging my horses' legs and brushing their hides, saddling them for the exercise riders, and sending them out to the track; cleaning their stalls while they were out, bathing and cooling them down when they returned, grooming bodies and bandaging up legs when they went back in their stalls.

I had some good horses along the way. I loved all my horses, even if they couldn't run fast. I loved the bond we developed. They looked to me for everything—food, understanding, entertainment, appreciation, empathy, love. I knew which horses needed toys to play with to stave off the boredom of twenty-three hours a day in a stall. I knew which horse liked her butt scratched. I knew which horse didn't like apples and carrots, so I bought her cherries, strawberries, and grapes instead.

Nobody is closer with a racehorse than the groom—not the trainer, not the exercise rider, and definitely not the owner. I loved my horses, because they truly were *my* horses. I loved my job.

But oh, how I eyed those exercise riders. They worked shorter hours—five hours a morning; they made more money; they had one day a week off; and most of all, they had the excitement of getting on those powerful racehorses and galloping away into the golden sunrise. Oh, the thrill. I watched them, studied them, lusted after their jobs, and dreamed and schemed while I shoveled horse poop out of my stalls.

I met a girl, Terri, who also worked as a groom on the track. She wanted to be a jockey. I wanted to be an Exercise Rider. We both wanted to learn to gallop racehorses. So that first winter, when the track closed for the season, we were thrilled to get ourselves a job galloping racehorses for a trainer in his backyard.

Homer had a little "bullring" track, a half-mile oval on his farm where, over the winters, he broke young horses and started his older horses back in training.

Terri and I first started getting on the batch of two dozen just-turned-two-year-olds that Homer had bought in a sale. We had an excellent mentor in Boz, who'd long worked as an exercise rider on the track and as a horse breaker. He was gentle in his horse handling and breaking, and he didn't put us girls on anything we couldn't handle. We sat on the colts and fillies, first in their stalls, then rode them under the shed row of the barn, around and around, teaching them to go and whoa and turn left and right. After Boz or Homer deemed them "broke" enough, Terri and I took them out on the bullring track and bounced-spooked-trotted-stopped our way around a couple of times.

How I didn't fall off and break my neck, I'll never know, because even though I thought I was a good rider, hindsight has shown me it was pure luck and zero knowledge that I imparted to those young Thoroughbreds. But I thought I was quite on my way to my dream of being an Exercise Rider. I would hate to quit grooming for Ben Harris the next season, but I was pretty sure he'd let me exercise his horses instead.

Finally, the day came when Homer sent us two girls, the aspiring, almost-accomplished riders, out onto his bullring on two of his older Real Racehorses. It was a cold, wet day in February, and time for the older horses to begin their comeback training for the new season at Longacres.

Fred was his name. A thoroughly unremarkable bay, he was shaggy, kind, nothing special. He would be my stepping-stone on my way to getting my Exercise Rider's license in a couple of months. I would owe Fred so much. I would remember him for a long time.

Terri and I jacked up our irons like we knew Exercise Riders did—not quite as high as a jockey's, but higher than simple baby-breaking—and we pulled down our newly purchased jockey goggles over our eyes like we'd seen jockeys do, and guided our Real Racehorse mounts toward the track.

"Just hand gallop them five or six laps," Homer instructed us.

I was so excited I could barely inhale a proper breath—this was it!

We urged—rather insistently—our mounts into a trot. After half a lap, our goggles were too wet to see through, so we pulled them down under our chins, out of the way, like jockeys did. Our gloved hands were getting wet and cold on the reins, as we forced our fat and lazy horses to a rather erratic canter around the track. They'd been suddenly yanked out of their winter retirement, and weren't as enthusiastic as we ambitious riders were. Terri and I alternated squinting through raindrops and just keeping our heads down and hoping the horses would keep up a canter and stay on the track.

Our mounts were pooped after six laps of trotting and cantering (we never quite got up to a "hand gallop"), but not half as tired as my legs were from standing balanced over Fred's withers, like Exercise Riders did. Technically, we had not even "galloped," but nevertheless, I had galloped my first official Real Racehorse! I was now (never mind this was a little backyard training track on a farm) officially a gallop girl—a Real Exercise Rider! My knees were weak from the exhilaration (and fatigue). I tried not to show how utterly thrilled I was as I climbed off Fred and gave him a pat on his neck, like I'd seen Exercise Riders do. I tried to remember exactly when the racetrack office would open so I could apply right away for my Exercise Rider's license.

Next day Homer legged us up on our older boys again. The sun was out; it was a beautiful day to be Real Exercise Riders galloping Real Racehorses.

Terri and I smooched our mounts into a trot for half a lap, and then we urged them into an easy lope. Our horses were more motivated today. This was it—this was the ultimate vocation . . . but then something was not quite right . . .

Fred was starting to pull away from Terri and her horse. Apparently thinking that he was now fit, and having listened to Homer's instructions of a hand gallop, Fred upshifted into one. I immediately reacted, pulling on the reins, trying to slow him down.

Fred kicked into a higher gear.

And in that instant, my world shifted upside down, from right to wrong, control to impotence, ultimate dream to trampled nightmare.

Fred grabbed hold of the bit and took off running, and with him, he stole my courage. I was abruptly helpless and terrified. The harder I pulled, the harder Fred ran. Panic rushed in and pure fear filled the gaps. I was now flying along at forty miles per hour with absolutely no control over anything. Weakness began to seep through me, and despair.

COWARD!

Now, if I'd had time in such a seemingly dire situation to sit back and think for just a few seconds, I'd have figured out that Fred really didn't have too many places he could go except around and around the little track, and that eventually, much sooner than later, he'd get tired and slow down on his own. But thinking is impossible, and reason does not exist when your brain is in panic mode.

The panic quickly consumed my muscles—I could barely keep my fingers clamped around the reins to hold on, and my legs were shaking so hard they were about to collapse on top of Fred.

Through my tears, I only saw the ground whipping below me . . . The ground was safe. It would end this nightmare . . . I wanted off. *I just wanted off.*

As Fred sprinted along, I swayed. We flew around by the barn again, where Homer was standing outside watching us. I let the reins begin slipping from my grasp as I prepared to leap.

Homer's yelling voice sliced through the hysteria in my head: *"HANG—ON—MERRI—DON'T—JUMP—OFF!"*

In the end I was either too exhausted to summon the last bit of energy needed to jump off Fred, or else some instinctive preservation gene stopped me from falling off, or, I was too chicken to even do that.

Somehow, I clung to that horse until Fred, having had his spirited run that recalled some of his earlier glory days on the racetrack winning races, got tired and slowed down. Even then, I couldn't pull him to a stop. He slowed to a walk when he was ready, turned himself around, and walked back to Homer at the barn. He was done.

I was too.

Homer grabbed a hold of Fred, and I slithered off him, my legs crumbling as I sunk all the way to the ground, because they had nothing left in them to hold me up. I wanted to cry but was too abjectly embarrassed, and just had nothing left in me.

It was a terrible blow. I'd never been afraid of anything in my life, but this was irrational, intractable, prodigious fear. It was too overwhelming. I knew deep down that I would never find enough courage to shove this panic away.

I wanted to quit my job. I never wanted to face a racehorse again and climb on his back. But I couldn't just up and quit my job for being a coward. I went back to work the next morning, and Homer legged us up on our Real Racehorses again.

I sucked it up and told myself I could handle this, *I could get through this*. I rode with a death grip on the reins, keeping Fred's head cranked ninety degrees to the side so he could never get over a canter; I rode with the taste of metal in my mouth and bile churning in my stomach. I rode with fear.

I never climbed aboard Homer's older horse again.

I had to face up to it: the disappointment of being a loser. A failure. I was too scared to gallop horses.

Humiliating, absolute defeat.

A shattered dream.

I returned to Ben Harris' barn as a groom the next season, and the next four seasons after that, until Longacres racetrack shut down. I had worked up enough nerve two more times at a quiet training track to try galloping a horse, but though I'd had control of the horse both times, the terror was still there bubbling under the surface. Just thinking about it started my insides churning: getting legged aboard that horse, riding out onto the track, feeling the thick rubber reins in my hands, the horse picking up a canter, taking a cross with the reins on his neck as he started picking up speed . . . to a gallop . . . starting to pull on the bit . . . the beginning rise of panic . . . and crossing that threshold to a runaway . . .

The horses could feel my shot nerves. Heck, I could feel it when my heart pounded in my throat and my legs trembled on their back. A friend who'd tried to help teach me to gallop told me, "They may take off with you, but they'll always come back to you," but I was never able to make myself let the horse get up to those first fast seconds of the *"they'll come back to you and you can control them"* part.

I'd never gotten my courage back from that bay horse Fred. I'd finally had to admit that I just wasn't cut out to be an exercise rider. Everybody else could do it—Terri was doing it and was, in fact, going to become a jockey—but I could not.

But that was life. A dashed dream sometimes opened the doors to other adventures. The path lies before you and the riches are there when you hang on for the journey, though sometimes it takes a while and some head banging to change your perspective. Sometimes the journey *is* the adventure that becomes the dream.

I loved my job as a groom. I experienced six marvelous, exciting years. I had some wonderful horses, some that couldn't run a lick, and some that could. Chalk Box was my best pal, a multiple stakes winner, and Washington Champion three-year-old filly. Herman was my Ugly Duckling *(some* people mistakenly called her that) who turned into a Beautiful Swan that could outrun the wind.

Happy as I was, though, tiny jagged shards of the splintered Galloping Dream still stuck stubbornly in the depths of my soul: galloping full out, leaning forward in my horse's flying mane, urging him on, moving with his rhythm, soaring over the ground, thundering wind and hoof beats—not fear—roaring in my ears; with me in control. I suppressed the dream, because the bitter sting could still pierce.

But it still lodged there—tiny, dormant, but alive.

Chapter 2—Ireland

RIDING OUT

Okay. So I was a failure at galloping racehorses in Washington.

But what about Ireland?

Thoroughbred racehorses and Ireland went together like manes and tails. You really couldn't be in love with one without being infatuated with the other. If that weren't enough to convince me, besides the Irish racehorses and the famous Thoroughbred stud farms and racecourses, there were other things to consider: endless counties of green grass, standing stones, Guinness Stout, and the famous Irish hospitality. Ireland had long had some kind of mysterious magnetic attraction pulling eastward on my bones.

Besides horses, traveling had become another raison d'être. I'd been to Europe in 1989 (Paris was a specific destination, to see the Prix de l'Arc de Triomphe, one of Europe's oldest and most famous horse races), and I'd spent three months trekking through Nepal and India in 1991. When 1993 rolled around, my internal travel alarm was banging on insistently about another trip, and my feet were getting itchy.

Ireland was vociferously trilling its siren song. Besides, there were still those nagging buried slivers of that dream I had of galloping racehorses. So—why not gallop racehorses in Ireland?

I can't explain it. Maybe I thought it would simply be easier to do on the magical Emerald Isle. The horses would still be strong, but I would be stronger. I would magically be able to speak Irish and they would understand me better than American racehorses. Or I would simply be braver. Or the luck o' the Irish would be with me and keep the fear at bay. Maybe the sun would shine warm on my face and the wind would be always at my back, and maybe everything would just click. Surely, it was just meant to be. And who was I to argue with foreordination?

It didn't matter anyway, because I didn't stop to reason it out; and the fact that I hadn't ridden horses much at all did not factor into it. It was just a fact: I wanted to gallop Irish racehorses.

So, I traveled to Ireland, and I galloped Irish racehorses.

I took a roundabout way getting to Ireland as a backpack traveler: via Scotland, then Northern Ireland, then Ireland; but all the way I worked on my goal of climbing aboard Irish racehorses.

My first stop on the mainland of Scotland was with friends, who had a friend Ian (who didn't know me from the Pope), who had some racing connections, and I put a bug in his ear before I left the Scottish mainland and continued on my travels. I toured the Outer Hebrides and the Orkney Islands before sailing across the Irish Sea, and heading first to Londonderry, then Belfast, Northern Ireland, in the thick of The Troubles. The night after I left Londonderry for Belfast, a bomb went off in a pub outside Londonderry and killed ten people. The latest bomb had gone off in Belfast seven days before I arrived, killing ten and injuring fifty-seven.

For days, I hung around a Belfast hostel waiting for a phone call from Scottish Ian, who was kindly going out of his way, working on finding me a racehorse-riding job.

I also hung around Belfast because it was spellbinding. I was bewitched by the tired, worn city of strife, with its machine gun-toting police, and its tanks sweeping the streets with gunners looking down their barrels right at you while you rode the bus to the hostel at night, and its incongruously lovely people. I'd thumbed my way up the Northern Ireland coast before coming to Belfast, hitching rides and consorting with who-knows-what-kind-of-possible I.R.A. terrorists. They were all delightful, warm people who could talk horses. I couldn't understand how such bad things could happen to such good folks.

I finally did get the call at the Belfast hostel one day from Ian, saying he'd arranged for me to meet up with an Irish jockey in Dublin about working for his trainer. I said a fond farewell to Belfast and lit off for Dublin the next day; and now, here I was in Dublin, Ireland, calling this Irish jockey from a pay phone on O'Connell Street. My heart was thumping in my ears when he answered.

"H'llo?"

Breathless and trying not to sound too worked up, I introduced myself and squeaked out, "Ian said you might be able to line up a job for me with your trainer?"

I'm sure now that Pat heard some thrilled American girl babbling on the phone. I wasn't flustered from talking to an Irish steeplechase jockey, but from the thought of getting closer to my goal of riding Irish racehorses, although how would he know that? All he knew was that a friend of his, Ian, had called him, saying that I, someone Ian did not know, was looking for a job galloping Irish racehorses, and here I was, breathing excitedly in his ear on the phone. *Oh*, sure *she wants to ride*, I expect he thought, *don't they all*.

Pat didn't know me from the Pope either, but being one of those wonderful friendly Irishmen, he agreed to meet with me. "Come to the Curragh tomorrow. I'll meet you after the second race outside the weighing room."

The Curragh! He might as well have said, "Meet me at the Gates of Heaven."

The Curragh racetrack was Hallowed Ground—home of the Irish Derby, won by the likes of Nijinksy, The Minstrel, Shahrastani, Shergar, Salsabil, Old Vic, and Generous! The Curragh had been the headquarters of horse racing in Ireland since the first recorded race took place in 1727. It was over a hundred years older than our oldest continuous racetrack in America.

Needles of electricity shot upward from my toes and out from under my hat the next afternoon when I stepped off the bus onto the grounds of the Curragh. I inhaled the history of royal horseflesh and heard in my head the echo of the great hooves that have thundered down its homestretch. I reached under the fence to touch the sacred turf. I saw my first Real Irish Racehorses stepping onto the track for the first race, and I quivered. I would soon be riding one of these mythic beasts!

Immediately after the second race, before the horses had even pulled up, I was standing outside the weighing room, nervous, fidgeting, hoping Pat the Jockey would recognize me. I knew which one he was, because he'd ridden in the first race. When he finally stepped outside he said, "You the American?"

We headed to the pub for coffee, where we chatted a while, but, pleasantries aside, I was dying to get down to business, and tried to keep my voice coming pragmatically out of my mouth.

"I'm on a backpacking trip but I wanted to come to Ireland to ride racehorses so what's the work situation-do-I-have-a-job?" So much for my composure.

Michael O'Toole, the trainer Pat worked for (I'd heard of him!), was stabled near the Curragh and was willing to try me out around the grounds, Pat said, and maybe let me "Ride Out." Not gallop, but *Ride Out!* It even sounded more thrilling here in Ireland!

And just like that, I had a job working with Irish racehorses. Pat offered me a room in his flat that was empty for a week. I could come on down to the little town of Kilcullen, in County Kildare, on Monday. Where it was and how I would get there, I didn't know yet and I didn't care, because I'd be there. I would have crawled over broken glass to get there!

At the end of the exciting race day, the friendly Irish racecourse security guard sent me and my Yankee accent off with an Irish prayer, which went something like, "May the road rise up to meet you, may the wind be always at your back, may the sun always shine on your face, may the rain make flowers grow at your feet."

And I added my own verse: May I Ride Out on my Irish racehorse . . .

Monday: my first day of work in a stable yard in Ireland! My alarm went off at 6:30 a.m., and Pat and I left for work before seven, rocketing along the narrow country roads toward the Curragh in the crisp green morning, passing by a myriad of stables.

O'Toole's yard was big, white, clean, and busy. I watched Pat tack his first horse and quickly muck out the stall; and as he and five other boys Rode Out, I started helping Francis, the head lad, with mucking stalls, which sure seemed to be awfully messy. (I found out later, they didn't clean stalls at all on Saturdays and Sundays.)

I had become skilled and quick at cleaning stalls after having worked as a groom on the racetrack for six years, but I'd been away from the track for a year, and I was out of practice. I felt I was working so slowly, but one boy told me to slow down because I was working like a demon. Michael O'Toole told me to slow down. I guess I was embarrassing them, trying hard to prove myself a valuable employee, one that might be worthy of Riding Out.

The lads were nice enough, and though I was the only female around, they didn't care one way or the other that I was there. They swore, they laughed, and they told raunchy jokes to each other like stable hands the world over. I couldn't understand half of what they said anyway.

They did probably think I was stupid. English is my first language. It is my only language. But I could *not* understand the English that most of these Irish lads were speaking. I sure *felt* stupid, always saying, "What?" to everything anybody said. They all looked at me as if I were daft, probably assuming I was mentally slow—after all, why *else* would an American girl want to work in an Irish racehorse stable? Most Irish *boys* didn't want to work in an Irish stable. I finally decided, after saying "What?" for the third time in response to the same question or statement that I would then just answer "yes": "What? What? *What?* Yes." I will never know what all I agreed to, and they sure gave me some strange looks.

I ended up not Riding Out my first day. Maybe it would happen tomorrow; maybe later. I didn't know. If I would have admitted it, which I most certainly would not, deep down I thought that some of these horses did look rather big and strong and imperious and intimidating. Perfect suspects for runaways. But I loved the Irish horse smell, the soft horse noses, the slick coats kept under rugs, the delicate and powerful legs, and shapely, sleek muscles, all under a bright sunny sky, in crisp winter air, on the green grass of an Irish stable by the Curragh!

After just one day, I'd worked up a blister on my foot, skinned my hand, built up a stock of sore muscles for the rest of the week, and strained my right wrist. I was whooped. I felt like I'd done a good day's work. We finished up at 12:30.

"Not bad for a Monday," I thought I understood Francis to say.

I gripped the car door handle in a subdued form of terror as Pat and I hurtled in his car toward home (Pat told me he'd wrecked two cars), and there I cooked dinner for Pat and his flat-mate Michael. I smiled and nodded, "Yes," at Michael a lot when he talked, because I couldn't understand anything he said, either.

Afterwards in the dark, I took a stroll around Kilcullen. With a current population of seventeen hundred people, it was two miles from the scene of one of the first and bloodiest battles in the 1798 rebellion against English occupation. Now the only battles were over which pubs to hit first.

Which we did before bedtime. It's what you did in Ireland.

We'd done the same the previous night after I'd arrived at Pat's: Went Across For a Drink. Which, in Ireland, does not mean going out to "a pub" for "a drink." It means going to every pub in town and having *a* drink at *every* pub. I was seeing Irish stars by the time I had hit the sack before my first day at work.

I learned fast. I couldn't drink like the Irish. This night, I started my drinking with half-pints. We still hit every pub, and I had a drink in every pub, but only wee little ones.

Back home, I passed out immediately, knackered from a first real Irish day's work with Irish racehorses and a full night's Going Across with the locals.

Three more days passed at O'Toole's yard where I didn't Ride Out. I wasn't exactly upset about it. It was either clear and very, very cold, or misty, damp, and biting cold, the kind that worked down into your bone marrow and froze there unless you were moving. One day it poured rain and sleet. I didn't have proper clothes for staying warm or dry while Riding Out, so I was happy to wait a bit to get on my first Irish racehorse.

One morning after a few hours of work, Pat and I left the yard early: he was riding in the afternoon races at Downpatrick racecourse in County Down, Northern Ireland, three hours up the road, and I was going along.

As we careened along the road toward Downpatrick, I asked Pat what it was about being a jockey that he liked. He thought a minute, with a faraway look in his eyes.

"The kicks," he replied. "It's riding out there in a race, and you're coming up to this huge black fence in front of you. You're on a first timer, and as you get to the fence, you grit your teeth and think, 'Is he going to make it, or isn't he?' And he does, and it's the greatest. Also the speed . . ." he finished thoughtfully, as his car shot down the narrow road, past blurred scenery and slower cars doing the speed limit.

"You don't say!" I said, as my hand wandered covertly toward my seat belt, which I tried to snug tighter.

Ten miles along, the driver of a car speeding in front of us (*this* was disconcerting!) waved at us and gestured. Oh dear. Pat gestured back sharply, and both cars pulled over rather abruptly on the side of the road. I thought it was Irish flip-offs, and a real Irish, or Irish Republican Army, fight might ensue, and I sized up the floorboard at my feet, looking for a good place to duck when the bullets started to fly.

But Pat was only accepting a ride from them. It was trainer Victor and his jockey son Colin, offering to give us a lift, since we were going to the same place for the same reason. Victor was running a couple of horses at Downpatrick that Colin would be riding. Pat followed Victor to the next town and parked his car, and we climbed in their car with them.

If it were even possible, Victor's driving was *really* scary; scarier than Pat's. I looked out the side window so I wouldn't be so afraid anymore and I wouldn't witness the moment we were all going to die. (I learned this useful technique in Sri Lanka, and I highly recommend it as a stress-free way to enjoy a car ride in which you will possibly be killed in a fiery crash.) I answered introductions and questions without ever turning my head to look at anybody. Even Colin said later he had been scared!

While driving and not concentrating on the road, Victor picked my brain on racehorse leg care, since I had been a racetrack groom in America. I casually let it slip I was looking for work Riding Out for a stable in Ireland next week. I had to give up my room at Pat's place over the weekend, and therefore my transportation, and my job at O'Toole's; and I needed another place to stay, and another job, if I still wanted to pursue my dream of riding Irish racehorses. Which indeed burned more brightly in me, since I'd had my appetite whetted around those beautiful Thoroughbreds in O'Toole's yard, and Riding Out was looking iffy in the few days I had left there.

Victor said he was looking for a worker for his stable who knew horse leg-work, and he seemed really interested in having me come and work for him, though he had a funny way of actually not asking me to do it.

Thankfully, we made it to the races without totaling the car and all of us in it. The sun was out; it was a brilliant day at Downpatrick, a "roller coaster racecourse" as Pat called it, a nice little country track in Northern Ireland. Downpatrick claimed itself "the friendliest racecourse in Ireland," and I couldn't disagree. Everybody there gave me a smile or a nod like I belonged. Never having been on a jump course, I walked part of the turf with Pat and Colin up to the last two fences. I'd never jumped so much as a foot high on a horse. These jumps were up to four feet high, some of them topped by a wall of brush the horses had to crash through, and they'd be taken at a gallop.

They looked hugely formidable to me, but if you're a jockey who likes driving fast and has wrecked two cars with seeming nonchalance, and wondering if your mount was actually going to make it over a monster fence you were charging at, you'd probably have a grand time. I was nowhere near that brave or daring, and I did not feel the call to be a jump jockey. I just wanted to gallop a racehorse over the flat. I'd have to mention to the trainer, when I finally Rode Out on my Irish racehorse, that I would not be jumping over skyscrapers.

I actually held my breath as Colin and Pat both rode in the third race (Colin won), and Pat again in the fourth. Pat finished up the track in each race, but his horses made it over all the jumps. I considered that a victory in itself. It was a very different world, this jump, or National Hunt racing. The sport is ingrained in the national psyche: it originated in Ireland in the mid-1700's.

The drive home was another unnerving wild ride. I didn't stop looking out my side window until we halted in a little village where we had dinner and drinks at a racing pub. The owners of Victor's winning horse bought us all dinner, treating me like one of the family.

Of course, the night wasn't officially over until Pat and Michael and I Went Across in Kilcullen "for a drink."

I worked a few days more in O'Toole's yard, mucking stalls, brushing horses, and trotting out a horse or two on foot for inspection. On my last day, O'Toole handed me some cash, which I was not expecting. I was helping Francis sweep up when Pat came along around noon and said, "Are you ready to go?"

And that was my last day in O'Toole's Irish racehorse yard.

I caught a bus back to Dublin, still hunting leads for other racehorse jobs, still waiting to hear a "yes" from Victor. One day I took a bus to Navan racecourse outside of Dublin, where Victor happened to have a horse in the fifth race, on which his son Colin happened to win. I wasn't *really* sure I wanted to work for Victor, but I had to start somewhere. My fingertips were aching to stroke more Irish racehorses, and my hands clutched reins in my sleep in my hostel bed. And here was the perfect opportunity to corner Victor in a good mood, after a win. He'd be as pumped up as a winning prizefighter.

"Nice race, Victor."

He beamed from ear to ear. "Thank you! How're'ya getting on?" he asked, his brogue as thick as Irish stew.

We'd worked our way through the Irish chitchat, when I made up my mind and asked, "You still looking for help, Victor?"

"Oh, yes, come with me, talk to my wife Sheila; we have a flat in Grangecon you can share."

I stared after him as he marched away still smiling, my mouth hanging open.

Was that it? Was I really hired? I had another job? I found and talked to Sheila, and indeed, she instantly took care of things. It was as if she'd been expecting me.

"Oh yes, come tomorrow night to Kilcullen, and someone will pick you up and take you to Grangecon and your flat."

That *was* it! I was working in an Irish yard again! *This* time, I would gallop my Irish racehorse!

My new Irish digs: Grangecon, population, near as I could tell, about nine people and twenty-two horses. It had two pubs (one on the right, one on the left), a tiny "store" (which had fresh vegetables in the form of onions), a "post office" (approximately the size of a broom closet), and a pay phone in the street. I'd be sharing "my flat" with Victor's sixteen-year-old apprentice rider, Emmett.

When he picked me up in Kilcullen and dropped me off in Grangecon, Victor was a live wire, bustling around the flat doing this and rearranging that like he was a proud king fixing up his palace for a princess, not his little apartment for some common poop-shoveling, leg-bandaging, starry-eyed rider-wanna-be stable girl. Victor built a blazing fire in the fireplace (which Emmett later told me he never did once for him), and just as it was getting nice and warm and cozy inside, we all left. Time to Go Across for "a pint" to the pub on the right!

We played pool and drank beer; and I met some of the lads from the yard that I'd be working with. Brian looked a lot like his big brother Colin, with the Irish curly red hair. I had honorable intentions of heading home after we left the pub on the right, but instead I ended up with everybody in the pub on the left, where three old men played lively, foot-stomping Irish music on a banjo and two accordions. What with one thing and another, we didn't get back home and to bed until 1:00 a.m. I fell asleep by the fire in my new home of Grangecon, County Kildare, Ireland, counting not sheep but beautiful Irish racers jumping stone fences.

My reintroduction to working again in Ireland was a brutally cold winter morning that stabbed icy fingers right through my inadequate clothing; brilliant sunshine, Victor barking and yelling, lads swearing, relatively quiet horses who were apparently used to the chaos, and horse legs from Hell. I wasn't sure what my "leg expertise" was going to be able to do for these godawful looking Irish steeplechase legs.

With thirty stalled horses, we seemed to be in a constant mad whirlwind of activity, but nothing ever really got finished. Cleaning stalls, wheeling carts of hay around, tacking horses, Riding Out (the boys—not me), taking blankets off dirty horses and putting them back on damp and dirtier horses, sometimes with a layer of straw between body and blanket, to let the air circulate and dry the horses after a workout. It was too cold to give them baths, so they'd have to stay dirty a while longer.

We took a breakfast break around 10:30 a.m. I was more starved than I'd ever been in my life. We gathered in the entry room where juice, tea, toast and jam, and eggs that Sheila made for us were sitting on the table.

I never did get to Ride Out with some of the boys; already on this first day, I wondered if Victor ever intended to let me. I had the sneaking suspicion that was never in his plans from the beginning. We "finished" work for the morning around 1:30 p.m., although we just sort of stopped in the middle of everything that wasn't getting done anyway—stalls didn't seem to be clean and the hay carts were still full.

Colin drove Emmett and me home, where we ate lunch, then Brian picked us up at 2:30 and brought us back to the farm. Thence commenced more Riding Out (except for me), brushing horses (they were dirty!), leg wrapping (both legs and wraps like nothing I'd ever seen before), different boys still cleaning stalls (who were they and where the heck had they come from?), feeding hay to the stalled horses, and feeding hay to more horses in paddocks. Then the sky turned red in a brilliant sunset and it got bloody cold but we kept working on well past dark. It felt strange being there so late. How, with so many people, could it take so long to get things done? It was like trudging uphill on a steep sand dune—sliding back so far with every step that you weren't making any progress.

After the horses were fed their evening grain meal, that seemed to be the "end" of "work," though everything had seemed to just stop in the middle of . . . chaos . . . for the feeding. Brian drove Emmett and me home at 6:30 p.m. It had been a long ten-hour day, but at least we didn't start work too early in the morning.

I was ridiculously tired, but of course, Emmett and I finished off the night at the two village pubs. It's just what you did in Ireland.

The next day was what became the typical pattern for most of my days in Victor's yard—always hoping to get to Ride Out, but not getting to. Always Victor was the same, a high voltage wire and shrieking in a high voice, sometimes smiling with it, sometimes not, so you didn't really know if he was really mad or really happy with things. Always so much pandemonium, such flurries of activity, and yet so much standing around also went on during the day, I could have had the whole yard groomed and legs bandaged (if I could find said bandages) by the time the three boys went out on and came back from one ride. Different boys showed up and bustled and rustled and yelled; people suddenly disappeared for hours, including Victor. Where did everybody go?

Victor wanted horse leg-therapy miracles from me, "the leg expert from America," (as he fondly continued to proclaim to everybody), but already it was hopeless. Fat legs, legs with knots, sore shins, "ouchy" walking. These jump horses took their knocks hard. With all the snooping I'd done around the barn and tack room, I'd found only eight sets of standing bandages, which were also used to gallop in. They were all questionable. Not worth wrapping legs in, and certainly not safe for galloping in, or at least not to my American racetrack mind. As for medicines or liniments—I couldn't find any. I didn't have any tools to even start making a dent in the beat-up legs. And besides, the horses' legs would probably recover on their own, like they had before I'd arrived on the scene. Perhaps Victor had really hired me on for American comic relief, or sympathy for my quest.

The usual mayhem continued all day—times of hurry and flurry, and times of dead space; and in the evening, nobody was really doing anything. I wasn't used to this not working and getting things done so we could go home, although apparently it didn't pay to get everything done early anyway, because Victor wouldn't let horses be fed their evening meal until after dark. Still, I liked to keep working and finish.

I couldn't find the boys anywhere—*everybody* seemed to have disappeared from the yard. "Where the hell *is* everybody!" I grumbled out loud. "Dang it, I'll just go start haying by myself!" Somebody had to do it, and I might as well start, or we'd be there till midnight. The only other person around was Robert, who was kind of the barn foreman, and he couldn't find anybody either. He was stalking around the yard, cursing the missing boys all to high Irish heaven.

I walked into the hay barn, and looked for a pitchfork to throw into the cart full of hay. I'd need it to toss the hay in the stall feeders, but danged if those hadn't all been misplaced. Or more likely hidden by one of the boys.

Hoping I'd find another pitchfork on the way to the stalls, I started pulling the impossibly heavy cart out into the shed row. I huffed and puffed and grunted and cursed my way into the barn, wondering aloud, "Why the HELL is this thing so dang heavy?" I growled. "What do they put in their Irish hay, lead?" I even stopped to look at the wheels to see if they were flat.

I struggled to pull the cart past the stalls, and stopped to catch my breath, when out of the bottom of the cart popped Emmett and Brian, scattering hay everywhere. I screamed and jumped in fright, then we all died laughing. "What if I'd found a pitchfork and tossed it in there?" I squealed, "What if Victor had found you guys in there?" and we howled some more.

When Victor showed up to supervise the night feeding at 6:00 p.m., we were still giggling, but we didn't dare spill the beans when he demanded to know what was so funny.

Robert had the day off, only I don't think Victor realized he'd been gone all day. He bustled and blustered around the yard bellowing, "Robert! ROBERT? *WHERE IS ROBERT!*"

The boys snickered and disappeared and I hid in a stall while Victor marched around the shed row in his knee-high green rubber boots, trim spotless white shirt, and natty Irish tweed cap perched at a jaunty angle on his head. "ROBERT!"

I felt a bit guilty, and came out of hiding when he was on his third round of the stables searching and shrieking, and ventured timidly, "Um, Victor, it's Robert's day off, remember?"

"Oh, well, yes, I know that, Merri, you can take care of tomorrow's runners," he acknowledged with a grin, not bothering to explain all the yelling.

We had five horses running at Naas racecourse the next day. There wasn't much I could do except for brushing them, checking to make sure they each had four shoes on, and putting the best standing bandages on their legs that I could find.

I started brushing other horses in the barns—it kept me warm and out of the Irish rain. When it rains in Ireland, it doesn't mess around. The boys were Riding Out, and I had to admit that while I still had this terrible urge to Ride Out, I was quite glad it wasn't me out there, yet. I was kind of hoping for a warmer, sunny day, with birds chirping and good footing and horses that would be easy to gallop on such a perfect day.

The boys cut the last lot short since it was still pouring rain and Victor wasn't around. I didn't have to be told not to notice. They still had four more sets to get out after lunch, but work sort of petered out since it was still dumping cold rain. Such weather wasn't a great motivator for woman nor man or beast to Ride Out in.

We had all the stalls cleaned, horses brushed, and hay put out by five o'clock, and were ready to feed the evening grain meal. The boys had the feed almost mixed when Victor called on the phone. I was the unfortunate minion to answer the phone, and he told me to tell the boys to hold off feeding until he got there.

Great. The messenger was going to get pitch-forked. I reluctantly told the boys the news. They scowled at me, Colin started cursing, and they started feeding anyway. I knew this wasn't going to be pretty, so, I disappeared. I helped Brian give a few horses electrolytes and such, and I just puttered around in the empty out-of-the-way stalls, waiting for the Thunder-God to appear and the storm to commence.

And Lord a-mighty, did it ever. The boys had the whole barn fed, when Victor roared in and blew the barn away, boards and stones, ripping apart every remaining shingle and lad. He cursed and chewed and spit out everybody, making them empty out every single feed tub and re-feed his new way, because he had just spoken with a Nutritionist-Who-Was-God. The poor horses were so confused.

"Brian! *Where is Brian?*" shrieked Victor.

I bravely shoved Brian out of the stall in which we were hiding, and into the shed row into the onslaught, while I stayed "disappeared", hunkering down in the stall and bandaging a leg—or something. I petted the horse, I undid one of his leg wraps and re-did it four or five times. Fortunately, the horse was distracted waiting for his food to be given back to him, anxiously poking his head out the door watching the comical proceedings, so he paid me no mind.

Colin just up and left after the first few screaming fits.

"Colin! *Where is Colin?*" Fortunately, I think Victor forgot I existed or had ever worked for him. Emmett and I didn't get home that night until half past seven.

I was in awe of, and a little fearful for, these magnificent jump horses. They were big and strong, hardy and bold—they had to be, running a couple of miles and jumping over big fences like these that intimidated and overwhelmed me on foot. Now I was going to be in the thick of it, assisting with running the horses at Naas.

We had five horses running in five races. Horsebox driver Mick drove Emmett and Robert and the first three horses at 10:00 a.m. to the racecourse, a half hour away; I caught a ride with Brian and the next load. The stable area was a busy place, with horses from all over Ireland and Northern Ireland arriving and unloading, people walking their horses around, loosening them up, going into and out of their assigned stalls for the day. Victor stayed away with his owners, so everything was calm and quiet around our horses.

Colin rode one of our horses unplaced in the first race while I stayed with one of my favorite horses, Arty, who was running in the second race. Since I wasn't technically a groom, I wasn't supposed to be in the walking ring, but Mick slipped me a pass, and, looking like an Irish groom who knew what she was doing, I led Arty up to the walking ring for his race. It was like any other paddock at the races: people crowded around the rails, hunched over their racing forms, watching the horses, studying the competition; owners and trainers and jockeys huddling together in the ring discussing strategies; horses in various states of nervousness—dancing on tiptoes or placidly following their grooms around. Arty was one of the latter.

Another jockey rode Arty in the 2.5-mile steeplechase. The pair was up front until the last two fences, where the winner passed them.

Next, Brian rode a mare I called Happy Face—because she was always crabby—in the fourth race. I was in the stable area cooling down Arty by walking him around, listening to the announcer calling the race, when I heard that Happy Face had fallen going over a fence. It was stated casually as the announcer went on about the other horses still galloping, but I was shaken. They *fell?*

I couldn't just turn Arty loose and run to the track in panic, as I felt like doing. I had to just keep walking Arty around, and wait for the news. It turned out Brian and the mare were okay, but poor Happy Face, I thought, as I saw her being led back to the stables, she was going to be *really* crabby in the morning.

Colin rode one of our horses in the fifth race and finished up the track; and in the sixth race, a 3-mile steeplechase, Colin and Lady fell a few lengths from home. This time I saw it happen—a stumble, a jumble of flying legs and arms and bodies flipping like rag dolls over a fence—and I was horrified.

Nobody really seemed too concerned about Colin as they crowded around Lady on the track . . . but they didn't pay too much attention to her either. It was just another day at the races, I guess . . .

Fortunately, Lady got to her feet in one piece, as did Colin. Back in the stables, I unbandaged Lady's legs.

Victor used what many trainers here used for supporting bandages on the legs: Elastoplast. Evil stuff. It was extremely sticky, and since nothing was put on underneath the Elastoplast, it ripped hair off the horse's legs when you pulled it off, and it hurt them like hell too. "Ya Baaaaaaaaaaaaastard," I muttered, repeating my favorite and most useful Irish expression that I'd learned in the pubs, wincing as Lady flinched when I yanked the sticky stuff off as quickly as possible. *I'd sure like to rip these bandages off these trainers' hairy legs and see how they like that,* I thought darkly. I was in a mood after our horse and rider spills.

It probably looked to Victor's stables to be a bad day at the races, but I was rather relieved that both the jockeys I knew, and the horses I was really getting to like, were not hurt. Rough business, this jump racing. Makes galloping around a well-groomed, solidly-footed oval seem quite tame.

I still wasn't getting to Ride Out. Even when one of the boys unexpectedly didn't show up on a given day (they usually called in to say they were sick), and there were only two boys to Ride Out several sets, I still wasn't legged up on a horse. Perhaps this was due to a language barrier, I decided. "Ride Out" in Irish meant grooming/stall mucking/leg bandaging/hay feeding person.

After a busy chaotic morning, we took a tea break. I was starved. I was always starving here in Ireland. It must have been from trying to stay warm and trying to keep from being bored, because I wasn't working hard. Today I did almost *nothing*, which is a lot harder than having too much work. I put a few horses on the Exerciser—the walking machine. I brushed two entire horses, then brushed them again, and took my time about it. I hung out in a stall with my new buddy, The Judge. I wrapped on a few tatty leg bandages, and I made myself scarce when Victor came in the yard and yelled at those other boys for not doing their job of re-bedding stalls, or whatever it is they did or didn't do.

How did Victor, or how did they, know what to do? What all *did* those boys do anyway? Where did they go when they weren't here? A week here, and I hadn't seen the same thing happen twice, and I never saw them around much. Maybe the regular boys and I were not the only ones who hid out in stalls.

I'd given up on legwork. There was nothing for leg therapy here, not even soap, unless I dared sneak in the house and steal a human bar of soap from the bathtub, or dish detergent from the kitchen. The only thing in the tack room was some nasty Chino Unction—a thick ointment for keeping cow udders soft and healthy—I wasn't sure how that was supposed to work on hot and swollen or lumpy horse legs. Perhaps it did help in some way, but once you put it on, you couldn't wash the goopy crap off with plain cold water, which was all we had, unless I tried to sneak in the house into the bathroom with a bucket for hot water at the same time I stole the soap. Chino Unction was like Vaseline mixed with glue.

I at least taught one boy how to bandage legs in the proper direction one day, and he saw the reasoning in it and seemed to think it was a grand idea; but that went out the window the next morning when he showed up at work with a hangover.

One particular afternoon Victor was gone, who knows where, and we started feeding the evening grain at five o'clock. We finished up smoothly in half an hour, and Emmett and I were home in time for the Australian soap opera *Home and Away* that he was hooked on.

Naturally, at night we Went Across to the pubs before sleep.

Shockingly, and inconveniently, I was getting a cold. I tried to ignore it but a sore throat was scratching away at me. It was blowing a bloody Irish gale outside when Colin picked me up late at 8:30 a.m. Emmett had the day off. Victor had joined us when we Went Across the night before, and he'd gotten a bit tipsy, so thankfully Colin remembered to come pick me up for work.

We were all finished with the morning feeding and half the stall cleaning when Victor showed up at the stables. Still a wee bit fuzzy from his night out, he'd driven to Grangecon to pick me up (way late) and had found I wasn't there. He asked me how I'd gotten in to work.

"Oh, Victor," I winked at the boys, "I used my own two feet! I didn't want to be late for work this morning so I walked all the way in."

"Oh, okay."

The boys tried to keep from snickering. Brian had to duck in a stall to hide his laughter. I don't quite think Victor believed me but a grin snuck across his face, and he said no more.

We had three horses in the races at Fairyhouse racecourse that day, two hours down the road by horsebox. A biting cold wind was still blowing. It kept up all day—bitter cold wet Irish winter wind. It didn't take long in Ireland to gain massive appreciation for wool. I'd been warmer on ski slopes in Colorado at 11,000 feet in a blizzard. I took refuge out of the wind and shivered in our three assigned stalls for the day. Colin and Brian tacked up their horses, Ranger and Dancer, for the second race.

I used my borrowed out-of-date stable pass and got to lead Ranger to the paddock. Perhaps it's all the "Going Across" but no one pays much attention to protocol. Nobody was going to say anything to me today about a paddock pass anyway, because it was so cold. I had on a T-shirt, sweatshirt, and two borrowed jackets and I was still shaking.

It was so misty we couldn't see but the first and last hurdle and the finish line on the racecourse. Ranger and Colin were in the top three until the third to last jump, when they suddenly got cut off and dropped back. Between the third and second to last jump, Brian moved into second place on Dancer. He thought he had a handful of horse—then he didn't. The boys gave us the blow by blow of the whole race afterwards, because the rest of us had seen nothing but the start and finish.

It was too cold and windy to give Ranger and Dancer a bath—the wind blew the frigid water back on me instead of Ranger's legs I aimed for. We didn't walk the horses too long in the wind before putting them back in their stalls and throwing blankets on them.

I led Donavint up to the paddock for the fifth race, and we both puffed blue smoke out of our nostrils like dragons in the gusting mist as we paraded about the ring. As I led Donavint with Colin aboard out onto the course, Colin pried my ponytail, which was firmly and warmly tucked into my jackets, out and pulled off the tie. He wrapped it around his whip and rode with it that way. "For good luck," he winked. Donavint was just a little horse, tackling those big jumps. He ran a lovely race, finishing a fine fourth.

I didn't even try hosing him off back at the stables; we just walked and walked in the cold wind, Donavint following me around like a puppy dog, my head hunched down in my jacket and my hands shoved deep in my pockets, Donavint's lead rope draped loosely in the crook of my arm. These jump horses just amazed me—they were so strong and gallant, and yet so gentle. All heart, they were. All heart.

Merri, do this—Merri, do that—Merri, drop what you're doing and go get a rag and wipe off poor Donavint's nose. Merri, go get a head collar. Merri, will you go dress over Prince? ("Of course, never mind the horse I'm in the middle of bathing.") Merri, go do this. Merri, can you bring me that. Merri, where are those leg bandages? Merri . . .

What did Victor *ever* do without me? Days of frantic work whirlwinds that started anywhere and went nowhere, like whirling dervishes; and things still never seemed to get done. This place was like a Chore Black Hole. And I still wasn't getting to Ride Out.

Still no riding for me, always one excuse or another, and since I didn't see the situation changing, I suddenly decided I was leaving in two weeks and heading to England with my backpack. I sure wasn't, however, going to complain today about not getting to Ride Out, because a heck of a windstorm was wickedly toying with County Kildare, enhanced by sideways pelting rain.

Victor himself was storming around, marching in his knee-high green rubber boots, screaming above the wind, "Robert! Robert? *Where is Robert? Where is Brian?*"

I made myself scarce in a stall with brushes and bandages as three gloomy bundled up boys and a few poor miserable horses Rode Out in the hurricane-force winds and cold stormy downpour. This day I was not envious of their Riding Out. Not one bloody bit.

I wasn't the only sick one, with several of us humans coughing and sneezing. It didn't, of course, stop us from Going Across in the evenings. Irish beer was a good antidote for Irish colds, or so I'd heard.

Finally, I'd had it. Victor was gone after lunch, and I told the boys, "Dang it, I want to ride!"

Brian said, "So tack up!"

I was dumbstruck. "Really?" Was that all I'd had to do all along?

Colin had to leave anyway, so he handed me his helmet. Robert helped me tack up Chester, and simple as that, I Rode Out along with Brian and Emmett!

Now, for reasons still unknown to me, and, I don't know why I didn't even question this at the time—other than I was so excited to finally get to ride—Robert made me take off my glasses. I am pretty much blind without my glasses. I'm talking, I-couldn't-clearly-see-the-big-horse-ears-in-front-of-me blind. Brian and Emmett were two wavering stick blobs on two big fat blots that floated above the ground (which I could not see clearly) while riding beside me. I could hardly make out the rail of the round gallop we started out on (and I was on the rail), and I for sure couldn't see more than two feet in front of me on the straight gallop (a blob of green), on which I somehow happened to be in front. I hoped my horse knew how to steer and where to go.

I was riding in Colin's saddle, and the irons were so short I wasn't sure I'd last the whole ride after a short "hack" on the round gallop. Jockeys have some awfully strong leg muscles, and seeing as I hadn't actually ridden a horse in, oh, maybe a year, my legs were screeching in five minutes. I could ignore them, though, because I was screaming inside from the thrill of finally riding an Irish racehorse, even though I couldn't see any of it and it was rather painful. On the walk down the paved road toward the straight gallop, I was able to lengthen the stirrups a bit to ease the throbbing in my leg muscles. Still couldn't see anything, but my legs felt much better.

We stepped onto the soft straight gallop and off we went down the Irish turf, and here I was, blindly galloping along this track through the green paths of Ireland on the Irish racehorse Chester. He took a good hold and pulled on me a bit, and I got a bit arm-weary, but I wasn't scared at all. Possibly, because I couldn't see anything. In fact, Robert had cleverly picked the right horse for me—Chester was out of shape and didn't really want to go much faster than a smart gallop.

The cold sunny Irish afternoon blasted me in the face, and I couldn't stop grinning. If I'd glanced back, I couldn't have clearly seen the boys behind me. Besides the fact that everything was blurry, half the time I really *could not see anything at all*, period, because Colin's too-big helmet fell over my eyes.

I found myself fearlessly flying along at a comfortable gallop, balanced over Chester's great rocking chair withers, moving with the horse, cute American butt up in the air. When the helmet fell down over my eyes, I had to tilt my head back to be able to peek out from under it, which arched my back, which *really* stuck my butt up in the air . . . And I began to realize the real reason that I was leading the way despite the fact I was practically blind, and why I didn't see nor hear the boys behind me, was because they were quite occupied with the view that they had ahead of them. Ah, the clever Irish boys.

But that didn't matter in the least, because Chester, my lovely Irish racehorse, and I just cruised along. We pulled up and turned around at the end of the gallop, a mile down, and galloped back—the boys courteously allowing me to lead the way again—and the thrill was so beyond words that I'd finally gotten to Ride Out on my easygoing Irish racehorse (even though I really couldn't see anything), that I just about turned around at the end and did it again!

I didn't want to let on to the boys how exhilarated I was, so I kept it under my hat (which was still falling over my eyes), and I had to keep my mouth shut to keep from squealing with excitement. However, the boys could not have missed the huge smile plastered on my face.

After my ride, the rest of the day at work was wholly insignificant. I floated on air until we fed at five o'clock, quickly and smoothly since Victor was still gone, and we got home in plenty of time for *Far and Away*. I myself was getting a bit hooked on the soap opera, since Emmett had introduced me to all the characters; and I was finding myself more than a little cranky when Victor was the reason we missed the show most nights.

Emmett had a flat-cleaning fit—unusual for a young boy— and after we cleaned and rearranged the furniture in the flat, he needed someone to beat playing pool, and I needed some Irish medicine for my Irish cold; and to celebrate a momentous day, we Went Across for some pool and a pint. Back at home, I fell asleep dreaming of Chester and my first Irish racehorse ride.

We had six runners in at Punchestown racecourse. It was to have been my weekend off, and with my wicked cold progressing down into my lungs, in spite of all the Irish "medicine", that might have been a good idea. But I volunteered to work; I couldn't pass up a day at the Irish races.

The night before, Victor had made us all stay late at work again, always coming up with more things to do (and making us miss *Home and Away!*) then insisting he take us out for a drink. There were inward groans all around, and I was starved; but I figured if we had to go for a drink with Victor, he may as well feed us too.

"Are you buying us all dinner, Victor?"

"Ah, ahem—well—yes, of course," he said, and the boys elbowed me in congratulations. It turned out to be a hilarious evening, with Victor predicting, in a deliriously good mood, at least three winners at Punchestown.

Colin's girlfriend Sinead felt Victor's forehead. "Are you all right, Victor?"

By our third race, that prediction was obsolete, since four of our runners had finished up the track—*way* up the track. But it was a beautiful sunny day, with that special golden light you get only in

Ireland in the winter, with the rolling grass course surrounded by gentle emerald hills, and all around those gorgeous, muscular Thoroughbred horse bodies and the lovely charming lilt of the Irish accents talking horses. It was intoxicating.

In the sixth race, Colin finished fourth on Prince, and in the last race, Brian finished a decent fifth on That's My Boy.

I was all set to go back to the farm on the van with the horses and take care of them, then slip home early, but Victor said, "Merri, you can come back home with us."

I stifled an inward slightly wistful sigh, thinking of my warm bed, since I'd had my mind set on an early night of sleep for once. But I was in Ireland to enjoy the Irish horses and the Irish hospitality. I could get well and sleep later. If I survived my cold, which I now suspected was approaching pneumonia. But it was the much more charming strain: Irish pneumonia.

I joined everyone in the Owner's and Trainer's Pub, then went with the family to a cousin's birthday festivities, where I was just another one of a big family of Irish aunts and uncles and cousins and friends, albeit with a slightly different accent. While I could easily understand this group of Irish men and women, people kept staring at me after I spoke, and asking, "What? What?" And then they would smile and nod, "Yes."

Part of this Irish celebration included going to a disco. I hadn't been to a dance hall in fifteen years; the disco era in America had come and gone. At midnight, eight of us stuffed into Colin's little car, and off we went to a disco in town. I thought it was a hoot, but they all said it was a "Gobshite"—bad music and a strange crowd. That didn't stop us from closing the place down though, at 2:00 a.m. After the last song, everyone in the place stood and sang the National Anthem, the words all in the Irish language (Gaelic). I was impressed. I haven't been to many American discos (well, not any, really) but I suspected we Americans did not sing the Star Spangled Banner at 2:00 a.m. closing time after a night of disco dancing.

One of the cousins was supposed to pick us up at 7:30 a.m., from the family house where we'd all crashed somewhere in the Irish countryside, and take us to work at Victor's barn. But said cousin, who'd also been to the disco, didn't wake up till nine. None of us did. Uh oh. We knew we were going to be in big, big trouble with Victor, but the family insisted on feeding us a quick (much-needed) breakfast before we left. My pneumonia was hungry. Was it feed a fever and starve a cold? Or the reverse? What did one do for pneumonia? I could never remember.

We got dropped off at the barn at 10:30 a.m., expecting Victor to be waiting and the firestorm to commence. The boys slipped right into the yard and into some stalls, while Sinead and I hovered near the door of the house, afraid to knock or venture inside. Besides, I was sort of on a tightrope between employee, guest, and family friend, so I never knew quite which way to lean. And today was my day off anyway, but . . . I still felt that tiptoeing was the more prudent part of valor.

"Oh dear," Sinead whispered, "here's Victor!"

He swept up to the front door and opened it, as we braced ourselves for the fury . . . and Victor grinned. "Come in, come in!" he effused. "Oh, there was no need to rush over here this morning!"

Sinead and I gaped at each other in confusion, and staggered inside after this strangely jolly and hospitable soul. Victor stuck his head out the door and called the boys in—in the *house*, not the entry room—for a second breakfast. Sinead and I stared at each other, wide-eyed, whispering, "Who *is* this man?"

Victor even scrambled eggs for all of us, including Emmett, who could not believe he was (first of all) inside the actual house at the family table eating with us, and (second of all) eating scrambled eggs on toast that (third of all) Victor not only served us but (fourth of all) had happily cooked up himself.

Emmett whispered to me, "Victor's never scrambled eggs for me in the two years I've worked here!" What was going on? Were people in Hell wearing woolen sweaters?

Perhaps Victor'd had a good premonition. Three of our horses were running that day in the Punchestown races. I caught a ride there with Colin and Sinead. Colin wasn't riding, but I walked with him out on the course, and we stood right at a Double Bank jump during the running of the third race. This was a 4-mile cross-country steeplechase, over banks, timber, and brush fences, an amazing zigzag round-and-back course over all sorts of challenging jumps. It was thrilling, scary, and astonishing to stand right there as the horses hurled themselves over this jump, which looked menacingly huge to me. A few jockeys yelled, "AHHHH!" as they appeared over the jump—with an obvious, involuntary touch of fear—but nobody went down. The horses seemed to land hard—and almost tip over on landing—but they all kept on galloping to the next fence. I just couldn't have done it, blindly flying over such an enormous fence, not knowing what was on the other side, or if I would make it over.

The horses looped around the course and jumps, and then took this same jump again, this time in the opposite direction. One horse hit the bank, flipped over it, slammed into the ground hard, chucking the rider in the ditch, flinging my slamming heart into my throat. The horse thankfully was all right and got up and galloped on after the field—just another tumble at the races—as the rider was helped to his shaky feet.

Our horse Arty fell at the second fence in his race—I saw the fall on a television in the clubhouse—and I ran to the track. The jockey was cantering him back, and he looked okay—these horses were *amazing*. I wasn't so sure I really had the stomach for these races, though.

Ranger, another of my buddies, was in the next race with another jockey. Now that Arty had fallen (and, last week, both Lady and Happy Face), I was starting to get nervous about this jump racing. Flat racing could be scary enough without the colossal jumps to lift a weary thousand-pound body over.

Brian and I walked to the second fence to watch. As Ranger flew over the fence past us, he almost fell on landing. I gasped as the jockey lost a rein and Ranger's nose almost hit the ground. They recovered and galloped along in last place, and I noticed I'd stopped breathing.

I was still holding my breath as they approached the next fence. From our angle, Ranger seemed to almost stop before he jumped it—it didn't look good. We saw his haunches disappear over the fence, as did the rest of the field, out of our sight. But soon we heard Ranger's name no more by the announcer. He must have fallen at the fourth or fifth fence!

Brian and I took off running in that direction, but by the time the race was over, we still hadn't found Ranger. We could not see the horse *anywhere*. Emmett and Brian split off and ran to opposite corners of the two-mile round course, while Colin and I headed for high ground. I scanned the whole racecourse with the telephoto lens of my camera—no loose horse anywhere. Where the hell was my buddy Ranger?

We flagged down the horse ambulance driver, returning from following the horses on course, and asked if he'd seen Ranger. "No, but come on, I'll drive you down to one corner." Brian and Emmett were just reaching the other far corners of the grounds, and had no horse in tow.

Finally, we spotted Ranger in a narrow deep ditch up to his knees in water, behind a jump. It wasn't a fence he'd jumped in his race! We'd have never found him; you couldn't see him at all unless you were right at that fence on the other side. How the heck, or why he got in there—who knew. He had to be carefully maneuvered to get him backed out of the ditch. Ranger was a bit shaken, but thankfully only bruised. The nice Irishman with the horse ambulance gave us all, Ranger included, a ride back to the gate in his horsebox, as the next race galloped past us. It had taken us thirty minutes to find him. I was so thankful we found him in one piece.

I woke up feeling awful, with a chest-aching cough. It probably didn't help that I hadn't gotten much sleep, as usual. I had made it to bed by half past nine for once, a blessed feeling, and was in a wonderful deep sleep, when at midnight, BANG BANG BANG on the door. Five or six people, including Emmett—who I'd thought was upstairs sleeping—barged in on me, plopped down on my bed and on the couch, turned on the telly, and whipped up a roaring fire. Oh, my aching head!

Somebody made tea, thankfully, as that cures everything Going Across doesn't, and we all sat around and told stories, until finally, around 1:00 a.m., they left, and I passed out again.

It was Victor who picked me up the next morning to bring me to work (Emmett had the day off). "I'm tired," said Victor.

"I'm sick," I croaked. "Victor, this will be my last week working for you. And the main reason is, I'm not Riding Out."

"Ah, Merri, Merri," he chuckled, "there's nothing I can do about that."

I scowled into my jacket. Yes, he *could* have done something about it.

"I know you Rode Out the other day with the boys."

I didn't say anything, just kept staring out the side window.

I coughed my way through the morning work, and after tea, Victor told me to find some liniment to rub into Arty, who was pretty stiff after his fall in the previous day's race. That was easier said than done, me finding a bottle of liniment within ten kilometers of that barn.

As I was digging around the back of the shelves in the tack room, Sheila came out and said, "Victor wants you to Ride Out on Alabama."

"Now?" I snapped irritably. I was feeling crappy, and therefore a bit numb to the thrill of my dream of riding Irish racehorses. Evidently one of the side effects of Irish pneumonia is lethargy. I'd apparently pictured all of my rides like the first one— green grass, golden sunshine, a bit of warmth and—was this too much to ask?—a pair of lungs that worked without hurting.

Colin knew better than to send me out on Alabama, a fit racehorse; he helped me tack up Bavard instead, bringing me an extra pair of his boots, and his saddle with the stirrups lengthened for me. Brian jerry-rigged a chin strap on another helmet that fit properly. I kept my glasses on this time. I Rode Out with the boys again, feeling this time more like an over-worked, ill stable hand that didn't want to be there, rather than a dreamy girl with Irish horse stars in her eyes.

Once around the short round gallop we cantered, then headed down the road to the straight gallop. Okay, I had to admit it was a little exciting, and not in the least scary, though I did feel terrible. I galloped Bavard beside Robert, tucked in behind a wall of the other three boys, and the long straight gallop physically overwhelmed me, even though my horse wasn't pulling on me at all.

And then we had to gallop back. Much of it was a blur, and my muscles were completely exhausted when we pulled up. My lungs were aching when we got back to the barn, but it hurt far too much to cough.

I felt like crawling in a stall and fainting, but Victor told me to Ride Out again, and immediately I Rode Out with the next lot with Robert, Emmett, and Brian, on Phardante. The naughty filly whipped her head around at first on the round gallop, lunging from side to side and fighting with the bit. I don't know how I stayed on, but I was too fatigued to even worry about falling off. On the straight gallop, I tucked her behind Robert and Emmett, using them for brakes, with Brian following us, so she couldn't go anywhere, but I still felt energy slipping out of my muscles with every stride. Galloping back, I let her roll along beside Emmett, still tucked in on the rail behind Robert, with Brian behind us in his prime viewing spot.

With my glasses on today, I could see the beauty I'd missed on my first day of Riding Out, but now I was too drained to care. Fortunately, Phardante was fat and out of shape (the boys knew well how to pair me with the horses, bless them), so she got as tired as I was, and although I was knackered, she wasn't too hard to pull up at the end.

Most miraculous of all, I wasn't scared galloping Irish racehorses, just as I'd hoped. Probably it was because I was so sick, and very likely because none of the horses had run off with me—thankfully, the boys had made sure of that. If I wanted to try taking up galloping at home again, maybe this was the approach to take: wait for a bout of pneumonia, then hop on some lazy, fat, and out of shape racehorses, and position them behind a wall of horses and riders for brakes.

Thank God it was lunchtime, because I felt like dying, and I looked like it; and my head and throat and lungs only got worse later in the day. I prayed I wouldn't have to Ride Out again. How's that for a turn of events? The afternoon went all right until Victor showed up and started barking. Emmett ran to join me and hide in a stall, and then Brian snuck in to join us, and we let Victor yell at other people (I *still* didn't know who all those other boys were who mysteriously appeared and disappeared), while we whispered and whiled away the tornado. Brian and Emmett helped me finish bandaging legs—that is, we hid in stalls crouched down beside horse legs until Storm Victor blew over.

Grand. I felt just *grand,* as the Irish said. I was horribly achy and energy-less. I didn't want to ride; I didn't want to work; I didn't want to do anything at all but pass out for a few days—but after tea, Victor came bustling about most importantly, and told us all to tack up. *Groan.*

I got fat Phardante again and Rode Out with Brian and Robert. On the round gallop, within ten cantering strides, she ducked right out from under me and I flew right off. I landed on my feet and hung onto her reins, after which, of course, I could not get back on by myself. I have a two-inch vertical jump on my best days. And this was not one of my best days. Brian had to jump off his horse, leg me back up on Phardante, and then effortlessly and blatantly leap back on his horse like a graceful gazelle. Show off.

We rode the horses onward to the straight gallop where Colin was waiting; I was so thankful when Robert and I traded off our horses for Colin and Brian to gallop down the lane. We sat on the other two horses letting them graze, then traded them off again when Colin and Brian got back. I had a tired Phardante to ride back to the barn at a walk.

Although I was still feeling like a train wreck, we Went Across that evening (of course after watching *Home and Away*) to play some pool and drink Guinness. Could I help it that there were two pubs in our little village, and both served Irish cold medicine? It was late enough when we staggered home that I knew better than to look at the clock.

The roads were wet in the morning when Victor picked us up. Victor was a very fast driver in the best and driest of road conditions, and he didn't slow down for lakes. "We had a bit of rain last night. A few floods on the road. Like this one," he observed, as, *WHOOSH*—we blasted through it and the car hydroplaned almost into the ditch.

"I wonder how much we got," he continued, not noticing our near crash.

I gripped my door handle tightly and stared out the side window, watching the explosion of water bombs created by our car.

And the Irish days passed: brushing horses, haying horses, wrapping legs with no liniment and used bandages (it was always wet in this corner of Ireland, so they never dried if I tried to wash them and hang them to dry), a bath now and then for some of the horses if the weather warmed up a bit, putting horses on the exercise walker, and mostly trying to look busy—or better yet, just disappearing—when Victor was around. I still wasn't used to not doing real work all the time, and just "getting it done", then going home for the day.

When I disappeared from view, I chose the stalls with my favorite horses—Ranger, Happy Face, Donavint, and The Judge. They never seemed bothered by the constant racket and yelling and pandemonium in their stables, but they sure didn't seem to mind quiet time with me. I talked softly to them, petted them, and hugged their heads. They seemed to appreciate a girl in the barn who appreciated the stupendous effort and courage it took to be an Irish jump horse.

Bad cough, couldn't breathe when I awoke—and no electricity! This was so bad. I couldn't boil water for coffee. We'd had a windstorm overnight, one hundred mile per hour winds someone said. A couple of trees blocked the roads, so Victor shortcut to the barn on some private drives (going the same speed as he did on the actual road, of course). Bless that Victor, he was kind enough to offer Emmett and me hot tea and coffee in his house before we started work. With that, and after coughing up the lining of my lungs for an hour, I was able to function somewhat.

The three boys were Riding Out when Victor came out and asked me to saddle up Skippy and get on him and walk him around the round gallop.

Well. This was the first time Skippy had worn tack since well before his hind leg operation several weeks before. He'd cut his lower hind leg, it had gotten infected, and then it had been operated on. The ankle was the size of a grapefruit now, which I assumed was supposed to be an improvement over what it was, though it sure didn't look good now. The veterinarian said he needed to start light exercise.

Skippy looked bored as I tacked him up and climbed on him, but as soon as we set foot out the gate, he erupted like a volcano. He wheeled and spooked and kicked up his heels, walked sideways and danced upside down toward the gallop. He thought, and expected, that we were out for some serious galloping. I could never completely give him his head, or he'd have bolted into a run from a flat-footed walk, and I'd have bolted myself for America because Victor would have killed me.

Skippy thought this walking was totally bogus, he was an *Irish racehorse* for crying out loud, and the only version of "walking" I could coax out of him was a prancing, exaggerated jog in place, which surely wasn't good for his ankle. We circled the little track twice, and when I turned him around to "walk" back to the barn, he really went bonkers. He spooked at the same tractor we'd been by twice, squealing like a stuck pig. He wheeled, walked, and danced on his hind legs, and tried to break away from me. One time he whirled and threw in a terrific buck, and I almost came off him. It seemed he thought we were training for an Irish rodeo.

Victor had, of course, just stepped out to watch us the exact moment Skippy had bucked. He said to ride Skippy some more . . . "If you think you can, Merri, Merri," he chided, shaking his head. "He's never gotten anyone off; you'd be the first."

Great! I could make Irish history here! Victor said to take Skippy around the block, on the country roads to where they forked to Dunlavin. So we headed away from the yard, and it was a good half mile before Skippy finally settled down. He relaxed and started to enjoy himself, and then everything was so grand, sauntering along the Irish countryside, just me and an Irish racehorse who'd won over a hundred grand (Victor had told me many times), on a lovely Irish morning. I was sure Skippy was having one of his best outings ever, even if it was only at a walk, by the time we turned around and headed back to the yard.

At tea break, the boys said they were taking a few horses to the Curragh. The Curragh! I wanted to go—I *had* to go. It would be my last chance to go and watch horses work on the Curragh. Victor would probably say no, but I had to ask.

I summoned up the courage and blurted out, "Can I come along?"

Victor let out a great patronizing sigh, as he and the boys walked out of the kitchen, headed for the horse van.

"Merri, Merri . . . there's nothing for you to see, you can't take pictures because it's an army camp," yadda yadda.

I said, with a great sorrowful sigh, "It's okay."

It got to Sheila. "Oh, for God's sake, Victor, let the girl go!"

I grabbed Sheila and hugged her, and ran out the door after the boys and jumped in the horsebox before Victor could think of the proper riposte to this girl power ganging up on him. Squeezed in the front seat between the boys and Victor, we all had grins on our faces as Victor pulled out of the drive.

We drove to a big groomed grassy plot of land behind the Curragh racecourse and parked. Great grand Irish racehorses were working all about, galloping, jogging, and walking, singly and in sets, going this way and that up hills and on the flats. I stepped out of the horsebox, onto the Hallowed Ground. How many great Thoroughbreds had trained over this very piece of turf over the last two hundred years? And this time, I came to the Curragh as an employee, an honorary Irish lad, part of the toil and sweat, a groom of the horseflesh that helped shape the history (in ever so small a way) of this great historic land of racehorses.

Brian and Emmett unloaded the horses and climbed aboard two of them while Victor held the third one. I followed the boys and horses with my camera. They worked right past me up a hill, crouching low and still and smooching to their mounts, so close that the breeze from their efforts lifted my hair. When they came back, Emmett got off his horse, and Victor legged me up on him. His name was Highly Suspicious.

"Ride him over that way and walk him around to cool him off." He sent me away, over a little hill and out of sight, because I had no helmet, and I had no business out there on a horse.

I was stunned. My mouth was hanging down to my ankles as I rode off because—

I WAS RIDING AN IRISH RACEHORSE ON THE CURRAGH!

I might as well end the story here. Fond as I was of my Irish horses and Irish boys, I'd already planned to move on, and instead continue my backpacking travels. I'd galloped my Irish racehorses (regardless of how out of shape they or I were), and I'd ridden on the Curragh, *the Curragh for Crissake!* (Even though I just walked.) Victor had given me an amazing gift that just couldn't be topped.

My last day in Victor's yard, I went to tell my favorite horses goodbye. I knew several of them would miss me, and wonder where their American girl went. I would miss them. I would worry about them.

On my last evening in Grangecon, I Went Across and met everyone in the pubs for the last time. It seemed that everybody had extra family that had come to see me off. We had a few beers, played a few games of pool. I won my last one, (nothing short of a miracle), and nobody cheated. I told everybody, "See ya next time."

I slipped out, and walked back to the flat. I didn't want to think about leaving—so I didn't.

I felt a part of the village, part of the family I worked for: part Irish. I daresay I'd made some big dents in a few Irish people's lives, but my God, they left some big craters in mine. It was grand, being a small part of their lives for a time, and I was filled with gratitude for my Irish family who had helped me achieve my dream of galloping Irish racehorses.

Chapter 3—Zimbabwe

RACING IN THE RAIN

"Hello and welcome to Zimbabwe!"

The barefoot man wearing a suit spread his arms wide and upward to mirror his great smile, his white teeth huge in his black face, as we slogged by him in the downpour. That seemed to be his job, standing in the rain, welcoming foreigners to Zimbabwe. We all shared a laugh.

Two things you could count on in Zimbabwe if you wanted to ride a horse: it will rain, and the phones will not work. It will rain, it will pour, it will deluge, and you will get soaked through your raincoat, as you trudge around looking for a working phone. You may find many telephones in Bulawayo city from which to call a horse riding place and book a ride; but most of the telephones will not work. Especially when it is raining. The other telephones will have long lines of people waiting to use them.

The Zimbabwean people are anxious to help you out. They don't like to say no. They don't want to disappoint you. They may help you by directing you to a hotel with a phone that will work in the rain and that will not have a line; but not only will you not find the phone, but the hotel will not exist. The promise, however, will have made you feel better for a few moments, which means they succeeded. They made you happy.

And in any case, you don't fret; you just smile at the welcoming Zimbabwean man, and laugh as you walk in the downpour searching for a functioning phone.

I'd arrived early that morning in Bulawayo on the overnight train with a group of four backpackers I'd traveled with for a month. I was *obsessed* with the idea of riding a horse in Zimbabwe before I left Bulawayo, and German Hubertus and Danish Lena were willing to come along for a ride.

My plan was to call KweKwe, a place recommended in our Lonely Planet book (also known as the Traveler's Bible), for horse riding. For a backup plan, we also tried the tourist office. These places were generally quite friendly, if not always particularly helpful, and this one was no exception. The amiable lady handed us bus and train schedules to KweKwe, and she gave us the phone number for Tshabalala, another stable. "No problem," I said, brochures in hand, we would call and book a ride—I would finally get to ride a horse in Zimbabwe, and yes, we would have a nice day!

Next stop: the post office to buy a phone card with which to use a phone. No problem—perhaps we'd even get to ride horses *today!* The phone cards in Zimbabwe were easy to use—plug them in a proper card-phone and dial the number. Phone cards were great, that is, when a phone was available. After buying a Zim$50 phone card, I went to the four card-phones in the post office: the queue was one to two hours long. Bloody hell!

We stepped outside the post office, and it was raining again. We walked to the bank to exchange money, a half-hour ordeal just about anywhere you went in Africa. After feeling rich with new money in fists, we walked hopefully back to the post office, but the line had not shortened one bit. Apparently, once you *did* get your turn on the phone, you took your time talking on it, because you didn't want to stand in that line twice.

Remembering the tourist office lady had said to go use the phones at the Selbourne Hotel ("tell him I sent you"), we sloshed around town looking for the Selbourne.

When we finally found the hotel, we couldn't find the entrance. When we finally found the entrance, we saw a sign that said, in English, "No Public Telephone."

Pretending we couldn't read English, we asked a man working in the Selbourne if we could use their phone: "The lady from the tourist office sent us."

He broke into a big smile. "Oh, yes! We can call for you, but we don't have a direct connection, but we can book it for you if you want to wait."

No direct connection, but they can book? What did they do—run down to the post office and stand in the two-hour line to call for us?

"But," he continued, smiling happily, "the Crazy Inn down the road to the left has a phone."

Next stop: the Crazy Inn, to use the phone, so that I might finally make a phone call about riding a Zimbabwean horse. We splashed along in the downpour. We passed the joyful Zimbabwean man in the suit once again, standing under a roof now, and again he spread his arms wide and upward, and smiled big, "Welcome to Zimbabwe!" We all laughed again.

On to the Crazy Inn . . . only we couldn't find it. "Down the road to the left," the man had said—how far? Two blocks? Two hours? Two countries? Nobody we asked knew where the Crazy Inn was. Perhaps that was an inside joke, a "Crazy Inn with a phone" for crazy foreigners.

We finally stopped on a corner in the rain, tired of this runaround. We decided to go back to the post office and just stand in that line. Which was still one to two hours long. Dadburn it!

Hubertus asked a local, who said there was another phone around the corner, in the building for paying phone accounts. There were only five people waiting for this one phone (why?), so we stood in line. After half an hour, hard to believe, it was our turn! *Finally*, tired, wet, slightly perturbed, I was a phone call away from riding a horse!

I called the Tshabalala stable that our friendly tourist office lady had recommended and held my breath: nothing! No ring, no answer, no nothing. I tried again, and nothing. Dead. Maybe it was raining at Tshabalala and their phone wasn't working.

I tried dialing KweKwe: it rang! Someone answered! Success! Only the someone was a recording in heavily accented English: "We're sorry. This number is not in service. Please consult your directory or try an operator." Dadburn it again! I tried dialing zero for an operator—nothing.

"Argh!" I hollered. Four hours, and not a single thing accomplished, except that my willpower was drowning in the rain. Was it really worth all this?

Hubertus and I walked back to the tourist office, where the friendly lady saw my dejected face and offered to call Tshabalala for us. After ten minutes of trying, she told us the number wasn't working. (Really?)

Somewhere out there, a Zimbabwean horse was waiting to carry me on a ride, but not today.

Back out into the rain, Hubertus headed to the hostel, while for lack of anything better to do, I continued slopping around Bulawayo. Normally I enjoyed exploring a new city in a foreign country, but I was too distracted by my horse riding aspirations, and wandered rather aimlessly until I stopped at the Grass Hut for a sandwich.

The sun came out while I ate, but as I left the café, it started raining again. There were now grade three rapids in some of the roads. I squelched through in my sandals, hoping fish would not bite my toes, while my poncho kept the rest of me damp. The four-phone room in the post office still had an hour-long line; it was 5:00 and they closed at 5:30. It looked like I might never be able to make a phone call in Zimbabwe. I might get to talk to these horse riding stables faster if I swam there in the rain. I plodded back to the hostel.

In the hostel bar, I dolefully informed my fellow travelers that I'd been unable to call about horse rides. They commiserated, knowing how important it was for me. A white guy leaning on the bar named Crazy Mike overheard me, and he said he just happened to do horse tours through a game park. (*Sure* he did! Perhaps he was also the owner of the Crazy Inn for crazy American tourists.)

It was a smaller game park than the bigger and more well-known Matopos National Park, Crazy Mike said, where you were likely to see rhinos, baboons and monkeys, and which had the largest concentration of leopards in the country.

Mike was a good honest salesman. "Ours is a rhino park, although we haven't moved the rhinos there yet. And it has every other wild game around here, except there's no elephant, no giraffe, no leopard . . ."

I didn't bother to ask what animals they did have. Wild game was irrelevant. I'd seen all that earlier in Namibia and Botswana. Crazy Mike had *horses* to ride. I got the big sales pitch on the "military-trained horses," blah blah blah; I didn't really care what he had or where he took us or what we likely wouldn't see—I just wanted to ride a horse! Lena and Hubertus still wanted to go also.

"Okay! We'll see about tomorrow," said Crazy Mike. I didn't set my hopes too high, because I wasn't completely sure he was genuine, having rather magically appeared like he had, and I knew it would be raining tomorrow in Bulawayo, and the phones would not be working again.

I woke up to bright sunshine, a great morning for a horse ride. But Crazy Mike, already at the bar in the hostel, said, "Tomorrow would be better." He was doing a different driving tour today, he explained. "It'll be better riding tomorrow, if the sun dries things out."

"But we want to go tomorrow, shine or rain," I insisted.

"Yes, of course. I'll pick you up at eight in the morning." Another thing you could count on in Zimbabwe, was that nobody will tell you no. I still didn't know for sure if Crazy Mike *really* had anything to do with horses.

Because it miraculously wasn't raining, the phones worked in Bulawayo, and there were no lines of people; but the phones for the horse riding places still did not work. Another disappointing, aimless day passed in my Zimbabwean quest for the Holy Grail: riding a horse in Africa.

The next morning Crazy Mike showed up at 8:00 a.m. at the hostel to pick us up and take us horseback riding—it was really going to happen! A few people had errands to run, and by the time Mike ran a group of us into town to the bank, the post office, the phone (!), the travel agency, and the store, it was half past ten before we left for the game park. I felt my riding time was ticking away, but, we were on African time, after all, where you weren't supposed to look at a clock.

At the game park, we were served a quick breakfast of coffee, bread, butter, and jam prepared by a friendly cook named Mavis. The horses were brought in and saddled up, and it was already 11:30, though I was trying hard not to look at my watch, and to think of the time we were wasting. My butt was itching to sit in that saddle!

Along for the ride, including me, were Lena, Hubertus, a first time rider Pete, Claudia, and our three Zimbabwean guides—somebody with a guinea feather in his hat, Owen, and Sebastian, who appeared somewhat loco but not quite on the same plane as Crazy Mike.

It was nice and sunny like the previous day, so I rolled up my sleeves and left my rain poncho in the van, and carried my backpack with my camera and lens and binoculars inside, since we were riding into a municipal game park.

Crazy Mike reiterated, "We have every wild animal here! Oh, except elephant. And buffalo. And cheetah. And it's a rhino park, but the rhinos aren't here yet."

It was noon already when I put my foot in the stirrup and mounted up, and *finally* I was on a horse, which I'd been denied for one reason or another, for three months in Africa. I was going for a ride!

Her name was Shantiqua, a pretty (but not so happy) pinto mare. Crazy Mike restated, "These are all military trained horses!" Was that why she was unhappy? Maybe she didn't have a good military career. Maybe this tourist riding career was a step down. Maybe she did not like not seeing Big Game in a Big Game Park that didn't have much Big Game. But, she went along fine, and we got along well enough.

We rode out into the bush with Owen as our head guide. This wasn't, even if we had been in a stocked game park, the prime game-viewing season. That was in June, July, and August. And with all the rain—I just couldn't believe Zimbabwe was in a drought—the winter bush was thick and green, and game would be darn hard to spot. Elephants could have completely disappeared twenty meters away, not that there were any elephants to see. And not to mention the obvious: it's hard to keep a group of eight people quiet.

As I'd learned to do in the Okavango Delta, I stuck right next to the guide—he was always the first to spot the game—and Shantiqua insisted on holding second position anyway. It was great fun for me, walking along through the bush, searching carefully, pretending to be a big hunter, picking our way carefully through the thorn thickets like the aptly named Wait-a-Minute bush, with backward thorns that grabbed you if you were careless enough not to recognize them. I knew them now. I had one of those thorns from the Okavango still buried in my elbow, and one from the Sossusvlei sand dunes still lodged in the bottom of my foot as souvenirs.

Shantiqua seemed to know that we were looking for game: her ears were pricked forward with interest, and she appeared to be searching the bush also, though not in a frightened or spooky way. The group behind me was being too loud for us to realistically approach anything, not that we expected to see anything, so it was a minor miracle when, in the distance, Owen, and then I, spotted a herd of tsessebe (southern African antelope). The antelope stood alertly and unmoving, watching us; and as our group noisily caught up and gawked, they quickly turned tail to run, with one wildebeest in their midst.

Wild African game! In a wild game park with no game! Seen from horseback! It was an added treat on my horse ride in Zimbabwe.

Throughout our ride, I talked to and patted Shantiqua, stroking her neck, fingering her mane, but she remained impassive and aloof. She never objected to me being on her back, or to anything I asked of her. She was indeed a well-trained horse. She was just doing her job, but had no interest in getting chummy about it.

We rode on in the bush, a big blue rain cloud making a beeline in our direction, and I tried not to think of my poncho I'd left behind. How many afternoons had I been in Zimbabwe now that it had rained? Every one of them? I tried to ignore the rain, but that didn't help. It started sprinkling, slowly, teasing at first; then it got harder, big bold serious African raindrops bulleting downward. Shantiqua wanted to turn tail to the hard drops, but we kept on walking, our heads down, big drops thudding like African drumbeats on our bare heads.

The deluge came; we were all soaked in a matter of seconds. On the plus side, at least my sweats and gray T-shirt were getting a good much-needed wash!

Ignoring the torrent (there was no lightning or thunder, and it wasn't cold, so it was refreshing), we walked and trotted on; and belatedly, Guinea Feather decided we'd run for shelter. *What's the point now after we are all wet?* I wondered.

Our group picked up a trot, which quickly shifted to a canter. My inner calves were already hurting pretty badly from the uncomfortable saddle design (was this what the military had to ride in? Maybe this is what made Shantiqua cranky?) with the stirrup leathers rubbing against them. My stirrups were too long, so I just stood in the stirrups on my tiptoes.

Our canter became a gallop through the fantastic downpour. Water, water everywhere! Falling from the sky, getting kicked up with mud from horses' feet, splashing in our faces. Shantiqua and I were fourth in the charging pack, and the spray of water in front of us as we all raced through a long deep puddle was awesome, a colossal fountain of great earth-quenching, drought-satiating, fresh, clean African rain. I *loved* it!

Shantiqua and I could see nothing but a great waterfall, spurting down and spraying sideways and shooting upwards. If one could come back in a later life as an African rainstorm, put me down for that.

Shantiqua was surefooted and didn't once hesitate, even in the blinding cascade, as we flew down the road. I balanced over her back, pushing her on, howling with pleasure, and I think that Shantiqua was finally having a bit of fun too. Somehow I think that this had nothing to do with racing for shelter; we were running just to race in the rain!

We ended up at the little entrance to the park, where all of the humans and horses comically crowded under the little shelter. We waited twenty minutes that cut into my riding time—who cared about a little shower when we were already soaked! It was enough time for the rain to ease off and for us to get a bit chilled. After I grabbed my poncho out of the van, we mounted up and cantered to our lunch spot, Shantiqua in her favored second position behind Owen.

There we unsaddled, turned the horses loose in a pen, and waited around for lunch. The food would have been ready, but the downpour had doused Mavis' fire, though she had tried every which way to save it. So we waited, still a bit chilled, as Mavis re-warmed the meal, and we told stories to pass the time. I put my poncho on, after the fact, but at least it blocked the wind.

When ready, lunch was a salad (minus the lettuce) and sadza—the staple food of Zimbabwe made of cooked corn meal—and delicious ostrich stew with mushrooms and spinach. It was a perfect comfort meal for a horse ride.

After an hour we saddled back up (Shantiqua didn't want to be caught), mounted up, and rode off into the bush again, with it still lightly sprinkling. I stayed fairly warm under my rain poncho, despite my clothes underneath being wet.

We found giraffe tracks—giraffe! Mike had said there were no giraffe here—and Owen said he'd seen one not far away from there that morning. We searched for it and tried to follow the tracks, but we couldn't find the big beast. Hard to believe we could lose giant giraffe prints in the mud, and not spot that tall neck somewhere, but it remained hidden. Sticking close to Owen again the whole time, and staying quiet whilst the other ones behind us yakked away, Owen and Shantiqua and I surprised, fairly closely, two wildebeest, which took off in a whirling splash of mud. We circled round and tracked them a while, but never caught sight of them again.

And then, we were heading back to the gates of the park. It had lasted four hours, but, what—our ride was already over with? I was hooked. A mere four hours had only whetted my thirst for more. Maybe Shantiqua and I could melt into the bush unnoticed for a few more hours.

We rode on out the gate of the park, and Sebastian said those who wanted to gallop back to the ranger yard could do so. Of course, I wanted one last exhilarating gallop through Zimbabwe.

Pete and Owen stayed back as the rest of us went on, jogging along the trail, then breaking into a gallop once on the dirt road. It was breathtaking, barreling along the wet road through the bush—until from one of the two horses ahead of me, I saw a human dangling. Oh, *no!* I thought, as the nearest horse bumped into them.

I slowed Shantiqua to a canter as I saw Sebastian, our guide, hanging off his horse's neck and trying to stop her. I pulled Shantiqua to a halt, which helped Sebastian's horse slow to a stop, and he let go of his horse's neck and landed on his feet upright, holding onto her reins. Sebastian's saddle had turned over and slipped back in mid-gallop! (I'd fortunately remembered to check my cinch before we left the lunch stop).

My mouth was hanging open in horror when I caught up with Sebastian, but crazy Sebastian was laughing, a great Zimbabwean smile lighting up his face. *Welcome to Zimbabwe!*

I laughed and stayed on Shantiqua, holding his horse while he re-saddled. Shantiqua wanted to go-go-go, and impatiently danced in place, scattering little rain droplets with her prancing hooves. Sebastian climbed back on, and then I let Shantiqua go; and together, my little African mare and I galloped, ran, raced down the road in the African afternoon, kicking up one last rainstorm in our wake, with the sun shining golden around the purple storm clouds, until we caught up to the others.

As we walked the horses back into the yard, I stroked her neck and whispered, *Thank you my lovely Shantiqua, for the best ride in Africa.*

Chapter 4—Washington State

I stumble into the barn in the dark and cold at 4:30 in the morning, barely awake. I am greeted by five heads staring out of their stall doors, listening for my footstep, looking for me to appear around the corner. Stormy blasts a whinny at me loud enough to wake the entire backstretch, then withdraws back into his stall, satisfied that I've arrived and his world hasn't come to an end; that his morning on the racetrack will now be routine.

I greet them all with words and a touch. Two more horses deep in their stalls barely flick an ear as I quietly slip in to unwrap their bandages and check their legs. They're like me, definitely not the boisterous early-morning types that all racehorses are rumored to be.

It will be a busy morning. According to the training charts prepared by the trainer the previous night, all seven horses will gallop. The "Gg3/4" by Joey's name stirs my adrenaline. It's his final major 3/4-mile work from the gate in preparation for his first start in sixteen months coming off a bowed tendon. I'm always nervous when Joey works. And, Stormy runs in a race tonight, which means my nerves will be shot at the end of this long day. But I can't even think about that now. I have a lot of work to do in the next seven hours.

The morning is a blur as I ready my horses for exercise riders, send them out to the track, clean their stalls while they are gone, and catch them as they return to the barn. One by one I bathe them, snap them by their halters onto the walking machine to cool down from their exercise, water them out until they've had enough to drink, and watch them for stress or injuries, while getting the next horse ready for its gallop person. My layers of clothes disappear as I begin to sweat in the cool morning. My coffee gets cold as it sits untouched on a straw bale.

There's a half hour break for the exercise riders mid-morning while the tractors smooth out the track; for me there's no time to rest. Joey will work first after the break, when the track is at its kindest, with no bumps or treacherous holes that he might stumble in at forty miles per hour.

I can't stand the pressure of watching, but I can't stand not to follow Joey to the track. He knows he's going to work. He knows I'm out there watching him. "Hi, Joey," I call to him from the rail as he warms up at a jog past me on the track, "Be careful." He bows his nose to his chest and prances, his tail lifted proudly, and he cocks his head toward me as he passes. I'm smitten and he knows it.

I stand apart from Joey's owner and trainer who are there with their stopwatches. From the grandstand, I watch as he breaks from the gate in the chute across the track. I am terribly tense, from my clenched jaw to my curled toes. Joey is an image of grace and power, fearsome and wondrous, floating above the track, gathering speed with every stride. He rockets around the turn into the homestretch. I try not to think of his cannon bones taking ten thousand pounds of force with every stride and those thin, fragile tendons precariously holding those bones to the muscles beneath a hurtling bullet.

As he careens toward me, I shrink, trying to be invisible so that my presence might not distract him. But there's no chance of that. Joey sees, hears, feels nothing but his joy of running. I'm overwhelmed by the tension, the excitement, the beauty, the raw power of my beast, when I sense something wrong. I glance to the finish line and my heart stops. A riderless horse is galloping full speed on the rail, *toward Joey*.

I am frozen to my spot; I can do nothing but watch. It's all a blur, happening too fast, though everything feels like it's in slow motion. Too late, I scream, "LOOSE HORSE!" but they don't hear me. Joey is running on instinct. The rider's head is buried in Joey's mane. Forty yards apart, the rider sees approaching disaster. She stands up on Joey and tries to slow him, but there's no stopping a roaring freight train.

A miracle happens. The loose horse swerves around Joey right before they collide. I about faint on the spot. My horse has still turned in the bullet work—the fastest time for the day at six furlongs.

Joey is very pleased with himself as he cools out, no concept of his near-death. I can't forget what just happened, can't stop my gut from quivering and my heart from slamming as I finish cleaning stalls and begin grooming my horses and massaging muscles and icing legs and applying standing bandages. My fingers tremble as I inspect Joey's legs, feeling his tendons and suspensory ligaments, searching for heat or the slightest swelling. But his legs are cold and tight. The trainer confirms his soundness before I apply a cool poultice.

The exercise riders are done for the day by 10:30 a.m. I am finished close to noon and I have a few hours' break until the second half of my day begins. I grab lunch and fall asleep on the couch in our office until my alarm goes off at 3:30 p.m.

Chore time: pick stalls, water and feed the starving beasts, each of which insists he or she is the hungriest horse in the barn and wants to be fed first. It takes a little diplomacy and bribery and sneaking around to make my seven horses all think each of them was the most deserving one who got fed first.

Stormy's not hungry—he knows he's running. He only picks at his grain. He's in the seventh race, which on this weeknight means he won't enter the starting gate until 8:30 p.m. Stormy is on Lasix, a diuretic; so once the vet arrives to give him his shot at 4:30, rules say I can't leave the barn. I settle down with a book to wait the hours out and try to concentrate on the words I'm trying to read, and not think about the race coming up. Stormy takes the wait much better; he stands in the back of his stall, still and waiting, saving up his emotions for the race.

Stormy had his bath in the morning and he absolutely hates being brushed, so all I have to do is run a soft rag containing baby oil and alcohol over his coat to make it shine. I comb a checkerboard pattern on his butt and tie a small braid in his mane for good luck. At the ten-minute call for the seventh race, I run his bandages and bridle him. The only things betraying Stormy's coolness now are his huge eyes and the occasional tremors that run through his muscles.

I lead Stormy to the paddock where his trainer awaits us for saddling. Stormy's owners are there also, expecting a big win. They won't get it because Stormy is in over his head again. They want him to be an Allowance horse, so they insist he run in allowance races—a step in class above claiming races—even though he will never be quite that good. This will be the last time Stormy's trainer humors them.

Even though we have no shot at winning tonight, as I watch my handsome horse warm up on the track, I'm terribly nervous. He will try his hardest because he knows I'm watching and because he has the biggest heart in the world. I am so lucky to have this horse, and in fact, the seven most beautiful horses on the planet to take care of, no matter how fast they run.

Stormy looks good for the first half mile, keeping his blinkered head and white nose in front of the field until the eighth pole, where the better horses pass him. But he hangs tough and will not give up and is only beaten by four lengths. He looks for me as he returns in front of the grandstand to be unsaddled, and I notice his back heels are raw from running a hole through his bandages. There are welts on his flank where the whip lashed him—as if he hadn't been giving his all in the last stages of the race.

With an arm draped over his neck, I tell Stormy how proud of him I am as we carry our battle scars on the long lonely walk back to our barn. His owners arrive and stand around with hands on hips, watching their investment, a bit disappointed again, no praise for his extreme efforts; ready again with all but the one correct excuse for him tonight—he was overmatched.

Stormy ignores his owners, nickers to me from the walker for a drink of water, for reassurance, to let me know he's cooled out and wants to stop walking in circles.

It's just Stormy and me left; his owners and trainer are long gone. I doctor his heel "owies" and run standing bandages on his front legs. It's getting late, but Stormy and I can't resist sneaking off to a meticulously landscaped grassy area that's off-limits to horses. I figure he deserves a treat after tonight's great endeavor.

By the time I hang Stormy's feed tub it's almost midnight. It's been a long day; I'm physically tired and mentally worn out and I have a half hour drive home. Even so, I can't wait to hear Stormy's good morning nicker five hours from now and to do it all over again.

Chapter 5—Washington State

THE ROMANCE WAS GONE

The romance had fizzled. The excitement was gone. It wasn't fun anymore. Used to be I looked forward to getting up every morning. Not anymore.

It had been a tentative decision for me three years ago, returning to this new racetrack, Emerald Downs, after the old Longacres had been bought by the Boeing Company and bulldozed. I'd landed a good job on the new track with a good trainer.

The first two years in Alana's barn at Emerald Downs were filled with wonderful horses that I groomed—and more worry. In my almost-three-year sabbatical from the racetrack between Longacres and Emerald Downs, things had changed. I still loved the horses I cared for at the new track, but I wasn't wearing those rose-colored glasses anymore. I saw things a bit differently now. Though it hadn't happened yet to horses that I groomed, horses broke down in races, and they were destroyed. I couldn't bear that happening to one of my horses.

And there was that big question: *What happened to my horses when they left the track; the horses I never saw again?* It was a fact that many racehorses ended up at the slaughterhouse. I didn't want to think about that. I had been able to ignore that ugly side of racing for a decade, but it was a blatant reality that now nagged at me, tore at my heart. I couldn't *stop* thinking about it now. Many owners consider their horses an investment; if they can't run and win money, they are no good for business. Tough decisions had to be made and the poor horses had no say in their destiny.

As a groom for Alana, the work had been hard but good, the people I worked with were fun, and I even got a day and a half off every week—a previously unheard-of concept that I learned I could no longer live without.

The big blow came when Alana had announced her retirement at the end of last year. All the horses I'd taken care of—fretted over, spoiled, loved—were gone, or dispersed to different barns; and at the same time Alana left, I should have called it quits too and retired from the racetrack.

I'd said a wrenching goodbye to my favorite horses. To Stormy. To Joey. A deep ache slashed through my heart whenever I thought of them, of how they must think I had abandoned them. To this day, I agonize over the look that Joey gave me when I loaded him on the van at the end of that year and said goodbye, not knowing if I'd ever see him again. He stared at me, tense, his head high in the air, his eyes huge. He knew it was over. *He knew.* I fled the van before bursting into tears.

I couldn't do this much longer—getting attached to horses and watching them disappear from my life, one way or the other. But I had returned once again as a racetrack groom at Emerald Downs because . . . because that was what I did. Like a growing bad relationship, I just kept going back, because I didn't have the sense or the backbone to walk away when I should have.

I still might have preferred to be galloping horses rather than grooming, but things were just not the same at this Emerald Downs track. All the old-timers said that, though they seemed to adapt better than I did. My former exciting aspiration of galloping horses had faded into the backdrop of a meaningless world of horse racing that I no longer had my heart in. My spirit was withering away. If I didn't have my dreams, what was the point of all this? And anyway, I still didn't know that I'd have the nerve it took to gallop horses on the racetrack in the mornings with all the other horses and riders out there. A runaway horse is still a runaway, and much more dangerous if you're risking other people's lives. So I was a groom in a new barn at Emerald Downs, working for a new trainer, with new horses to take care of, but I wasn't sure what I was doing here anymore.

And I knew some of my old horses were scattered about the barn area. Joey wasn't back on the track yet for training this new season.

But Stormy was. Four barns down, he lived in a stall in another trainer's barn. Not a hundred yards away. But I would not go visit him.

"You're going to end up with Stormy one day," my housemate, Lali, kept saying to me. She'd said it for the last two years, while I had groomed Stormy in Alana's barn.

"Oh, no I'm not!" I swore. I didn't have a farm or a truck and trailer. I didn't even have a home. I couldn't have a horse.

Don't get attached, I'd warned myself. I'd learned this painful lesson, over and over, for eleven years. So many times, I'd been left with a broken heart. But how could one *not* get attached to some of the special horses, when you spent all day, every day, with them?

Don't get attached. Forget Stormy. Life would be so much easier. So much less painful.

But I couldn't help it. I still loved Stormy. I thought about him a lot, and he was so close; but I would not go to his barn. He wouldn't have understood why I suddenly showed up briefly and then disappeared again. I tried to forget about him, tried to throw myself into my work at my new barn. The other grooms were fun, the trainer was fine, and against my will, I got attached to some of my new horses; but my heart was sputtering on empty.

I was always careful, when I was outside our barn—dumping manure, sweeping, walking horses—to make sure Stormy wasn't walking up the road to the track for exercise. I did not want to see him. I didn't want him to see me. I didn't want him to know I was here at the track, and not taking care of him.

But it happened. One day while I was out on the wash rack with a horse, there he was. Stormy and his rider were being ponied by his new trainer up the road past our barn to the racetrack. My heart tried to slam its way out of my rib cage. I was sure everybody could hear it booming. I shrank into the wall and held my breath, though Stormy could not possibly have seen me with his blinkers on and looking straight ahead. But when he was even with our barn, he stopped.

Stormy stopped, he turned his head straight at me, and looked me right in the eyes.

My heart exploded. My eyes filled with tears. *He knew I was here all along.*

I had to say something. "Hi Stormy," I croaked. He took a step in my direction, and I took a step in his direction, but the trainer on her pony, who hadn't heard me, had kept moving forward, and she jerked him along after her. Stormy watched me, swiveling his head, as he was led to the track, until he passed the barn and I was out of sight. I tried not to cry.

I quit my job a month later.

I never went back to the racetrack.

Chapter 6—Texas

ENDURING

It's all Al's fault.

The blistering sun. The pitch dark. The sweltering heat, blinding dust, terrifying thunderstorms, and the stinging sleet. Deadly rattlesnakes, biting gnats, icy rivers, treacherous rocks, killer bogs, and perilous cliffs. Thirst, hunger, windburn, sunburn, frozen fingers. Sweat and tears and despair. The bruises, scrapes, sore muscles, and smashed toes.

The shattered bones.

The godawful rides that last forever. The crazy horses that pull your arms out of their sockets for fifty miles. The crotchety horses that buck and toss you on your shoulder. The horse that bolts. The horse that tries to die on you.

It's all Al's fault.

Laughs and cheers and joyful tears. Six thousand miles of the best trails ever. A Tevis buckle. A French riding license. Wide, wild open spaces. Deserts, forests, canyons, mountain ranges. Pioneer trails. Hoof beats and heart beats in twelve different countries. Splendid snow, rain, sunshine. Wildflowers, wild animals. Solitude. Companionship. Partnership. Soulmates. The best friendships, ever. The best horses, ever.

I still wanted to gallop horses. Could not get that out of my heart. But I was still scared. Could not get that out of my head. But that enduring ache, that aspiring fantasy, drove me to try again.

Somehow, there *had* to be a way I could ride and ride and ride horses and revel in the power but not be afraid of it.

I didn't dare try racehorses again because I knew how that would turn out. But surely *somebody* wanted their horses exercised; horses that took you faster than a boring walk, or took you out of the confined arena, but that didn't run away with you. Something in between and sane. Was that too much to ask?

I walked into a local tack shop in north Texas one day, told the proprietor Al I wanted to find a job exercising horses, but not racehorses.

He didn't hesitate. "Why don't you try Shelley down the road? She does endurance."

"What's that?"

What is endurance, I had asked.

I went to see Shelley. She hired me. I never in a million years could have imagined the consequences of that fortuitous path.

Not only could I ride horses that (usually) didn't grab the bit and run off with me, but I could ride them *all day*. Sometimes all night, too. Endurance riding, I discovered, is a long distance riding sport that anybody could do. Old people, young people, daredevils, and those who wanted to be daredevils one day. The competitive. The restrained. The cautious. And it wasn't just a couple of miles that endurance riders rode, but 25 miles, 50 miles, 100 miles in one day. Or 250 miles over five days in a row. Pick your addictive bliss.

And to condition a horse to be able to do this, you had to ride them. A lot. The beauty of it was, since you rode so far in a competition, it was the rare horse that ran faster than you wanted it to. In fact, in endurance it didn't matter at all how fast you rode. Some people rode to win; some people rode just to experience the trails. The choice of pace for most endurance riders in America is the trot, a perfectly sensible way to cover a lot of ground efficiently. The motto of AERC (the American Endurance Ride Conference) puts it perfectly: *To Finish is to Win*. At most rides, you even won a prize for finishing last—the Turtle Award.

Another of the beauties of endurance riding was that I didn't even have to have my own endurance horse, because it's the rare person who owns just one endurance horse. If you already have one, it's always better to have a second one, so that you have a backup just in case the first one becomes temporarily lame. And somehow a third horse often seems to pop up in the same pasture with the first two—it's often inexplicable; it just happens. And when a person finds herself with three or more endurance horses, she rarely has the time to condition them all herself. Shelley was an endurance trainer—she had over a dozen horses that needed regular riding. A lot of riding.

So I got to ride, a lot. There was nothing particularly scary about it. We mostly trotted. A little bit of cantering here and there got me close to a gallop . . . just close enough to let me know that cantering was fast enough for me for now, where I still owned my confidence. And anyway, you didn't have to ride fast on a horse to learn how to handle one, how to understand him, how to control him with finesse. (Fifteen years later, I am still learning this.) And so I learned to trot—and trot confidently. For miles. For hundreds of miles over the years. Thousands of miles. Not in confining arenas, but over trails in the great outdoors over every kind of terrain, in every kind of weather, in every kind of situation. I learned to listen to my horses. I learned how to ride, really *ride*, as we covered those miles.

I met the best people while endurance riding. You can get to know a person and a horse well, riding with them for fifty miles. Often, though, the experience of this sport is so good that sometimes you don't even have to speak a word if you don't want to. Sometimes the grandeur of your surroundings, and the awesomeness of your horse, says everything for you, and you both understand that.

I met the best horses endurance riding, although there were one or two that presented certain . . . challenges . . . like one particular mare that bucked me off onto my shoulder at a disagreement on a fork in the trail, and one particularly frantic mare that pulled my arm muscles into knots, from start to finish.

But even in the challenging cases, with people and horses, the companionship in doing something so physically and mentally challenging together forms a special bond with them that you don't get when you go out for a five-mile trail ride, whether or not you speak in words.

And the athleticism of these horses was phenomenal. I grew up playing sports in school, and I'd remained active and fit since then, working on the racetrack forking all that hay and shoveling all that poop, playing sports, skiing, hiking, and building trails in the mountains. I thought I was athletic. But the Arabians that I rode—

the predominant breed in endurance riding—staggered my mind. They went down the trail with a mission, and they went, and they went. It seemed so effortless for them, and they were so willing. They took me further and faster to places I'd never have gone on foot.

Endurance riding is the Great Equalizer. It makes all people Normal. In real life, you can be rich or poor, old or young, short or tall, snooty or timid, a CEO, the king of a country, or a poop-shoveler, but you're all equal for one day when you're riding on the back of a horse for fifty or a hundred miles.

You don't have to have a $50,000 horse to ride endurance. Some good endurance horses have no papers. Some have been rescued from the kill pens. Some first roamed the West as free mustangs. You don't have to have a pretty horse. You don't even have to have a horse. A pony or mule will do. You can ride a Clydesdale or an Arabian or a mutt, and when you cross that finish line, in first place or last, and the veterinarian says your horse is fit to continue, you're still an endurance rider on an endurance horse.

It's a mutual partnership that has nothing to do with your income or job or how honorably you live. Endurance riding is not just about you. Whoever you are or however insignificant or high and mighty you may be, you have the responsibility of getting your four-legged partner healthily and safely to the end of a 25-mile or 50-mile or 100-mile ride. You can't fail to be astounded and humbled by the ability and the willingness of your most incredible partner. It is a privilege to ride an endurance horse that doesn't stop giving, ride after ride. If you don't think so, endurance is probably not the sport for you.

In this sport, nobody cares what you look like. That worked out well for me, since I wasn't known as a fashion plate. Anyway, what do you *think* you're going to look like after fifty miles under a helmet on a hot dusty day? You don't have to have polished equipment or tailored clothes, and your horse doesn't have to wear color-coordinated tack or perfectly matched, evenly spaced braids down his neck. That worked out well for me too, since I wasn't particularly renowned for my grooming techniques. The horses I ride like to get down in the dirt and roll after finishing fifty miles of trail. I let them, and I don't brush them afterwards. I like to dunk my head in a water trough when I'm hot and dusty. I don't brush my hair afterwards. A hat works well to hide Helmet Hair.

It doesn't matter how bent-over you walk, or how slowly you shuffle when you get off your endurance horse. It's no big deal if you have to ask someone else to trot your horse out for you at a vet check. Walking like a cripple after an endurance ride is rather like wearing a badge of honor. *"Can't walk, but I just rode a hundred miles!"*

My hero is an octogenarian 30,000-plus mile endurance rider, Julie Suhr, who, while she recently retired from long distance endurance rides, still gets in the saddle and rides several times a week, and still does Limited Distance rides. She may hurt when she dismounts, but she won't mention the discomfort. She'll only tell you how wonderful the ride was, and she'll mean it.

Try riding an endurance horse as therapy for physical and mental injuries. The more troubles you have, the sweeter the trail is. It all melts away for a while when your endurance horse carries you over one mountain range and across the next valley.

On some endurance rides, you'll reach your own physical or emotional limit. Some days, riding fifty or one hundred miles can be one of the hardest things you've ever done. You'll want to quit. Some days you will quit.

You will ride again. Because that bond you form with your horse over hundreds, and then thousands, of miles is like no other bond you will ever have with another living creature. It's the closest thing to sacredness outside of religion. For some it is a religion.

Endurance horses have ultimately carried me through California, Idaho, Washington, Oregon, Utah, Texas, Arizona, Colorado; Malaysia, New Zealand, Australia, the UAE and all over Europe. They've taken me to meet princes, sultans, a sheikha, and a king, and lots of commoners just like me. But that's not what's important.

The acute longing to wrap my fingers around the reins and look between the ears of my endurance horse to the trail beckoning ahead of us dominates my existence. I crave the adventures with a revered equine partner, effortlessly covering the ground, carrying me through wild spaces, cantering along the ridges, racing the thunderstorms, following the curve of the hills, dancing through the forests, skimming the deserts, and conquering the mountains.

Julie Suhr put it succinctly: "A horse makes me feel ten feet tall."

Riding an endurance horse puts me on the top of the world.

It's all Al's fault, and if I ever run into him again, I'm going to thank him.

Chapter 7—Washington State

THE VISIT

He just wasn't into it anymore. In just a few months, he'd tumbled in class from $20,000 to $3,200 claiming races, the very bottom of the ladder for cheap horses running at Emerald Downs.

Stormy went about his routine, like racehorses do—training, racing, eating—but it didn't mean anything. Nobody spent time in his stall hanging out with him. Nobody fed him apples and put the stickers on his doorframe. Nobody told him he was awesome or beautiful anymore. Nobody really cared one way or the other. He was just a tool used to try to make money in the racing business—and he wasn't making much of that anymore. He not only didn't count, he was becoming a loss.

In May, he stumbled at the start of a race and dumped his rider. The reins went with the rider—flying over his head. Stormy raced after the field and stepped on his reins, jerking his head down savagely. He kept running, a loose horse mingling with the sprinting herd to the finish line. When he was caught by an outrider after the race was over, blood was pouring out of his mouth.

Back at the barn, it was found that he'd almost severed his tongue. He had a number of stitches to reattach it. It left an impressive scar.

He was claimed in August out of a race for $3,200 and moved to a new barn. He lost his next three races, and was taken home for the winter by his new owner-trainer Chris—who was, coincidentally, or by divine intervention, the daughter of Alana, the trainer I'd worked for while I had groomed Stormy. At Chris' farm, he developed a knee infection. As he was healing, he grabbed a front quarter of his hoof on the same leg while clowning around, and at the same time he popped an abscess out of the same foot.

And so it was that Stormy's right leg was bandaged from elbow to over the hoof, and he was quite lame, when I went to visit him at Chris's farm. He looked like a battlefield casualty.

I hadn't seen Stormy in over a year—not counting that one accidental brief encounter on the backstretch of the racetrack before I quit—but it was as if he'd been expecting me. He was staring out his stall door, listening for my footstep, looking for me to appear around the corner; he recognized me the moment I stepped in his shed row. He nickered at me. When I laid eyes on him again, all my buried emotions of attachment erupted to slap me upside the head.

We had a wonderful reunion. I hugged Stormy's head, I planted kisses on his nose; I took him outside his stall without a lead rope, and he wouldn't leave my side. It was as if we hadn't been separated for over a year.

I smothered that warning fire blazing in my head, *Don't get attached.* I stomped it out and threw the ashes to the gods. Contrary to all reason—I still had no place to keep a horse; I still had no truck and trailer; I still had no home, and I still couldn't afford a horse—I tried talking Chris into selling him to me.

"You don't want Stormy anymore," I reasoned shrewdly. "He'll be eight, plus he can't run any cheaper, and it will be hard to get him back into shape again for another season of racing . . ."

She wasn't interested in selling him. Not yet. "Maybe after next season . . ."

I was sort of secretly relieved to hear that, because it was a crazy fantasy, and I had no idea what I would have done if she'd said yes. The brief daydream faded with a whimper. The end of next season was a long time away. This was likely the last time I'd ever see Stormy. If that's how the gods wanted it, then that was that.

When it was time to go, I took off Stormy's halter. He tried to put it back on, sticking his nose back in it.

When I walked out of the gate, I shut the gate on his shoulder, because he tried to follow me out.

As I walked to my car, I felt his gaze boring a hole in my back.

I turned to look at him. He stared hard at me. He started pawing at the gate.

Sometimes horses can see things we humans can't comprehend. Stormy knew something that I could not yet see.

I would not turn back and look at him as I drove away, and I would not blink, so the welling tears would not fall from my eyes.

Chapter 8—Texas

ROCKY START

Montell Cliff Hanger 3 Day Pioneer Endurance Ride
3/19/99—32 starting, 29 finishing
"Winner: Wind Swift Barak ridden by Melde, Merri in 04:52"

Our alarms went off early enough, but somehow, time slipped away and we were late saddling our horses for the 7:00 a.m. start; and we found ourselves scrambling, trying to get to the starting line on time. Something so simple for Shelley, who'd been endurance riding long enough for the whole process to be as automatic as brushing her teeth, but I was more than a little flustered. Wait! Where were my gloves? Where was my fanny pack? I forgot to fill my water bottles! Where were Rocky's brushing boots?

Time mercilessly ticked away, indifferent to a newbie endurance rider who would have preferred a leisurely, calm start. "We have to go!" the veteran Shelley called. We tightened our saddle cinches one last time. My nerves fluttered and my heart felt like popcorn kernels banging around a hot popper—it was my first endurance ride!

The horses were amped up and ready to go. Both of them, owned by some Arab sheikh and trained by Shelley, were competitive and used to finishing in the Top Ten, and they often won their rides. They knew they should have already been at the starting line warming up and swirling around with the other horses. I was worried that I might have a handful of horse at the starting line, and I wasn't *that* great or confident a rider. Shelley jumped on a bouncy Pharrah, and I gathered Rocky's reins and clambered on his dancing back with two minutes to start time.

As I settled in the saddle, I instantly discovered something awry: my stirrups were too long! "Wait!" I yelled to Shelley. I jumped back off Rocky to raise the stirrup leathers as he twirled around me, while Pharrah crow-hopped impatiently around us. But now things were worse than amiss: my stirrups *did not shorten!* This was disastrous!

One important endurance proverb I hadn't learned yet was to never, *never* try a new piece of equipment or clothing the day of an endurance ride. I had ridden Rocky before, but I had never ridden in Rocky's special *saddle* before. Shelley had long, long legs. I did not.

"Shelley, wait!" I screeched. "My stirrups—!"

"They're about to start! Let's go!" yelled Shelley, and she was off to the starting line!

Rocky jigged anxiously around me, urging me to get on with it one way or the other, and since I didn't know what else to do, I jumped back on him and chased after Shelley and Pharrah. We arrived at the starting line just in time to hear, "Trail's open!" and take off down the trail in a clustered herd of excited horses and riders, and *I couldn't reach my stirrups!* "Help meeeeeee!" I yowled in harmony with the "Yeehaws!" and "Whoas!" and horse snorts and hoof beats.

As we jostled for position on the trail, I bemoaned to Shelley the somewhat dire fact that my stirrups were too long.

"We'll be back to camp in a couple hours and you can change saddles there," she responded, the problem quickly resolved and forgotten, as her eyes squinted in concentration at the competition ahead of us. *A couple of hours?*

Obviously, this was no big deal. Probably this happened to endurance riders the world over every weekend, and you just ignored it and shut up and rode, flopping around in the saddle like a fish on a bicycle!

Shelley uttered this statement about the exact time she spied her Big Rival up ahead. Shelley's competitive spirit kicked in and our game plan suddenly upped an ante or two. "Come on! We can catch her!" she yelled, ignoring my floundering legs.

I could barely reach my stirrups at the trot even if I stood on my tiptoes. Now we slipped into a canter and I couldn't grip them at all! My butt began sliding around in my saddle like melting butter on a hot skillet. *Now* what was I going to do? I couldn't just scream at Shelley to stop—we were on an endurance mission! I couldn't just stop by myself and . . . what would I do anyway since I already knew my stirrups wouldn't go any shorter? But I was too overwhelmed to be afraid and too flustered to figure out anything else to do but to hang on and pray.

I grasped Rocky's reins and mane with one hand, and with the other, I clutched the saddle pommel with an iron death grip, and tried not to slide right out of my leather seat. If Rocky spooked or tripped, I was a goner. I would fly right off, and Shelley and Pharrah and Rocky would never see me again until the ride was over later in the day. But that wonderful Rocky was very steady and balanced; he knew his job, and that was cruising straight down the trail, no matter what the flailing monkey on his back was doing.

Shelley and I cantered side by side on a two-track road, kicking up dirt clods behind us as Big Rival always just disappeared around a turn in the trail ahead of us while the central Texas forest swept by at a blur. My foot muscles started cramping as my big toes stretched downward, desperately seeking the lightest caress of the stirrups. My thigh muscles started cramping as I used them to hold myself as centered on Rocky as possible. I tried to guess how long this first loop was going to last, but I couldn't even recall how many miles long it was.

The trail dragged on and on forever, before we finally came to a turn-around point at a post where we were supposed to mark our vet cards with a crayon, and then turn around and return on the same trail to camp. Before I could even pull Rocky to a halt, Shelley had jumped off Pharrah, marked her card, grabbed my card out of my hand and marked it. By the time I stepped onto the ground, Shelley thrust my marked card back in my hand and was about to jump back on her horse, because there was no time to waste!

She glanced down and said, "Oh no! Pharrah lost a shoe!" Apparently, that calamity far outweighed my lack of stirrups.

How inconvenient, in this madhouse! Horses roared up to the post and screeched to a stop! People jumped off and on! Wide-eyed horses neighed and snorted! Riders hollered! People and horses crowded around the crayons and jostled each other in close quarters! Shelley grabbed a rubber Easyboot out of her saddlebag and slapped it on over Pharrah's shoe-less hoof in ten seconds—I'd never been able to get an Easyboot on a hoof in ten minutes!

"High five!" Shelley yelled at me. "Let's go!"

Discombobulated by the mild bedlam, I reflexively threw a hand up, and by the time Shelley whacked my hand in congratulations she was back in the saddle and off at a canter down the trail, chasing Big Rival! I threw myself back on top of Rocky and gave chase, slithering all over my saddle. I just hoped I could make it back to camp. If I fell off, Shelley would never notice!

We met slower trotting riders on the two-track road as we cantered along. We zoomed around corners, ducked under branches, whipped over hills and dells—Big Rival was not far ahead of us now!

"Come on, we can catch her!" Shelley hollered to me over her shoulder. I hung on to Rocky's saddle and mane as I implored the Endurance Gods to give me a second chance at this next vet check if they let me get there, as we cantered after the leader, because praying seemed to have gotten me this far.

I don't know how I managed to stay on that horse for the twenty miles of that first loop. It lasted a couple of very uncomfortable, disconcerting hours. When we got back to camp, after we vetted our horses through the vet check and went back to our trailer, I immediately changed saddles on Rocky, to one I'd ridden in before, one in which I could reach the stirrups.

After that, the whole new world of endurance riding opened up to me.

On loop two, it dawned on me: "Ooooh, we're following *ribbons!* So *that's* how you know which trail to take!" I said.

Shelley laughed. She thought I was cracking a joke, but I'd really had no idea how anybody knew where to go on that first fast and blurry loop.

Ribbons, tied to trees or bushes, were all on the right. If you were following ribbons on your left, you were riding the wrong direction. If you weren't following any ribbons, you were lost—time to backtrack to the last place you saw a ribbon and start paying attention. There were even different color ribbons for different loops. Three ribbons marked a turn coming up. What clever ideas! We hadn't made it to the ride meeting the previous night, where you learned all these important things if you didn't already know them. Shelley, of course, already knew all this, and it wasn't comprehensible to her that anyone didn't.

We slowed down a bit on the second loop, mostly trotting and some cantering—even though we were still stalking our Big Rival. I now took much more notice of my heroic horse Rocky, now that I didn't have to concentrate on staying on top of him. Rocky was moving easily and comfortably, and the pace was not stressing to him. That was the biggest thing to know and pay attention to, in endurance riding. If you didn't take care of your horse, it didn't matter where you were in the race. Without your horse, you were nowhere.

Shelley's Arabian horses were fit. They'd passed the first vet check easily: heart rate, muscle tone, hydration factors, and gait were all satisfactory. After our horses had spent the required hour of resting and eating and drinking, we'd cantered out onto this 15-mile loop two, where I was now finding my wits and discovering the intricacies of a delightful new sport.

We would have another vet check and "hold" after this second loop; and after the third and last loop of fifteen miles, we would have a final vet check at the finish line. The horses had to pass the final vet check to receive a completion for the ride. This endurance riding was starting to make perfect sense—and it was fun! Now that I wasn't concentrating on not falling off, I noticed we were riding far out into the beautiful Texas hill country.

We stalked our Big Rival up and down those rolling hills. I learned some 50-mile race-riding strategies for front-runners (that I've never used since) on that day, and I learned some pointers on taking care of my horse during a ride (which I've used every ride since). It was an entertaining and educational cat and mouse game we played with the leader. We walked up the hills and conserved our horses' strength, and cantered down them, where our Big Rival could look over her shoulder and think we were chasing her down (which we were). We paused to let our horses drink in every creek we crossed, and moved right on if they didn't want water. If one was riding to win, you didn't have time to dally on the trail. We'd throw our sponges-on-a-string in the water as we waded through, squeezing the water down our horse's necks as we trotted onward, to help cool them down.

And I learned to pay attention to those ribbons that guided us along the right trails. It was easy to miss a turn if one was talking instead of watching for ribbons. At one point on the second loop, our Big Rival disappeared from sight. We heard later that she'd taken a wrong turn somewhere, and she ended up behind us.

That left Shelley and me in front for the last loop of the 50-mile ride. We were far enough ahead of the other riders that we didn't have to race those last miles. Since I'm not particularly competitive . . . or rather, since I have no competitive bones in my body, I had forgotten that the point of this race on these good horses was to win. I was more enthralled with the great fun I was having riding such a cool horse such a long distance. The possibilities looming in my imagination were running amok—there were endurance rides in just about every state in the country—in deserts, in forests, in mountains and by the oceans, during the day, sometimes into the night, in every month of the year.

After less than five hours in the saddle, my first endurance ride came to an end. Shelley and I held hands as we cantered across the finish line tied for first place. I'd won my first endurance ride!

Obviously, I had no idea yet what I was doing in this endurance sport, but *I wanted more!*

And I got more the very next day, where, on my second endurance ride ever, Shelley gave me another of her horses to ride named Masrita. Shelley instructed me to finish in about eight hours; Masrita and I crossed the finish line after eight hours and twenty minutes on the trail, trotting over the line holding hands with another rider, tying for last place, and winning one of those coveted Turtle Awards. I forget what I won for first place on day one, but I still have the key chain Turtle Award from last place on day two of the Montell Cliff Hanger. Despite the fact that the winner had finished four hours ahead of us, people in Ridecamp who saw us ride in cheered just as loudly for us Turtles that day for finishing last as they had the previous day, when Shelley and I had finished first. There aren't too many sports that praise you for finishing dead last.

I was tired after riding a hundred miles in two days. I was sore; I was utterly elated. I had become an instant endurance addict. I'd unknowingly stumbled over and fallen into my Dream Bucket.

There was more, much more to come. Through the good times and the bad, all around the world, the trails of endurance, viewed between the ears of an endurance horse, were now my calling.

MONTELL CLIFF HANGER 3 DAY PIONEER ENDURANCE RIDE
3/20/99—39 STARTING, 33 FINISHING
"33RD PLACE: MASRITA RIDDEN BY MELDE, MERRI IN 08:20"

Chapter 9—California

THE MOST BEAUTIFUL HORSE ON THE PLANET

I looked out my window at the Forest Service horse herd, huddling together under the willows against the biting bugs, out of the sun: Paiute and Tom, head to tail, swishing each other's faces. Zak and Redtop hovering close to them, catching a little of the swishing. Brenda the mule, Chino, and JD.

And one horse, standing by himself fifty feet away, in the hot sun, covered with welts from bug bites.

Stormy. My horse.

My horse.

I'd so badly wanted a horse when I was young. Nobody else in my family had the horse gene, as far back as I've been able to ascertain. My parents grew up with work horses on their farms, but there was nothing romantic about working horses in those days. They pulled plows, wagons, or carriages, and were only as valuable as their labor.

My oldest brother and sister were long gone from the house when I came along; my next brother left for college when I was five, and I have only faint memories of him at home. I was a "surprise" in more ways than one for my parents—born late in their lives, and born completely horse obsessed. I'm not sure my parents were totally prepared for either.

Drawing horse pictures occupied my spare time when I was six or seven, and they were published in our local newspaper. It was some kids' art contest that was held once a week; looking back, it was clear I was not much of an artist! Apparently, there weren't many children submitting photos from my small town.

As early as nine years old, horse racing was what got me started reading newspapers and magazines. I grabbed the sports section first thing every morning, and scanned it with the fervency of a bookie to see if there was any news on horse races. I cut out the articles and saved them. I got my hands on Sports Illustrated magazines and tore out the horse racing articles and filed them in manila folders. From what I can recall of my childhood, it is all categorized by racehorses—the year Cañonero II won the Kentucky Derby and Preakness; the year of Riva Ridge; the great years of Secretariat. Then Seattle Slew. The great rivalry between Affirmed and Alydar.

I could name all the Triple Crown winners and the years they did it. I watched the big races on television, and I recorded them on a tape recorder. Somewhere I still have those cassette tapes packed away, of Secretariat winning the Triple Crown in 1973; of Forego, the hard-knocking old gelding, winning the 1976 Marlboro Cup Handicap by a nose under an astounding one hundred thirty-seven pounds in the slop; of Ruffian in her match race against Foolish Pleasure in 1975. I still get goose bumps watching Youtube replays of those races.

Ruffian was my first true racehorse love affair. As young and unworldly as I was, (twelve) I knew she was a freak of a horse and I would see very few like her in my whole life. I knew she would win the Match Race against Kentucky Derby winner Foolish Pleasure. Instead, I watched her shatter a foreleg and break down. It was harsh reality for a horse-crazy little girl. I got up early the next morning to read the newspaper for an update on her condition, and I was stunned and devastated when I read she was destroyed after coming out of surgery poorly. Ruffian was the first horse I cried over.

I suppose some of this could be blamed on my older brother. He thought he'd be nice to his little sister when my parents and I visited him in California, and he took me to the morning workouts at Hollywood Park. I hung onto the rail, mouth gaping, stars in my eyes, as the beautiful Thoroughbreds galloped and worked down the stretch, and backtracked jogging by me on the rail. I gawked at those lucky, lucky riders as one might ogle movie stars. And when one boy jogged his horse so close by the rail, close enough that I could have reached out and stroked the horseflesh as he went by (if I'd been so bold), I gazed up at him with pure awe and adulation and smiled reverently. The exercise boy glared down sourly at me. I was in love. *I was in love!* He had *the best job in the world!* I knew from then on that I wanted to do what he did when I grew up!

I was around eleven when I first sat on a horse. My mother had relatives in West Texas; they had a friend who owned a couple of horses. The cousins took me to his barn for my first "ride"—i.e. to sit on a saddled horse. I remember not being able to make the horse do much of anything (smart horse), and the adults chuckling at me. The horse grazed a lot as I objected and tried to make him do anything else, like carry me around, but I still thought I was one riding fool.

It is indeed possible that one can become a junkie at a very young age, because from then on, I was completely, irreversibly addicted to horses. Possibly, I might have been deprogrammed if I'd never sat on that first horse, but my parents were unaware of the permanent damage it caused. After I "rode" that horse, it was too late. Horses bolted through my bloodstream and on down into my bone marrow, and there was no extracting them and no turning back.

That momentous first "riding" occasion started the horse ownership campaign in earnest. I never thought past "getting a horse" as to what I would actually *do* with it—feed it, pet it, ride it, love it—I just wanted a horse. *A horse of my own!*

On some mornings, when the equine pang was particularly bad, I'd get up early, read our small town newspaper, study the classified ads, pick out the best looking Horse For Sale ads, carefully circle them with a black marker, and pointedly leave the newspaper laying on the dining table for breakfast, folded to best expose the hint, moving everything else well out of the way so there was no mistaking the precisely placed newspaper. My parents never took the hint.

One particular morning I edged the newspaper back toward my dad's bowl of cereal after he'd pushed it away to make room to eat; as he edged it back out of the way, some discussion ensued which explained why we weren't getting a horse. I don't remember the words; I don't remember crying or having a tantrum over it. I just wasn't going to get a horse and that was that. I was disappointed, yes, but not discouraged. There is no discouraging a child (addict) whose mind is set on something that's already a part of them. They might as well have declared that I could not have a left leg.

As a sort of compromise, my father and I developed a routine: once a week, he would drive me around our little town in south Texas to visit the horses. I knew where all of them lived. I climbed through fences to get to them; I petted them, I talked to them. I fed them carrots. I named them all. I still remember two of them: White Star, a white mare, and Plateau, a white-faced chestnut gelding (I thought this was a particularly clever name choice, though I'm not sure I even had a concept of what a real plateau was). My dad twiddled his thumbs in the car until I was finished, and as we drove home, I'd already be planning what I'd tell the horses next time I came to visit them. It worked out pretty well for all of us: I got to be around horses more than I ever had, my mom and dad didn't have to pay for one, and the horses got treats.

I think we could have afforded a horse, but it just wasn't what young girls in our small town did. We lived in farming country, but nobody that I knew in school owned horses. Nor did I even know a single person who was obsessed with horses the way I was—and I knew just about every kid in the small town.

And then one day, as a twelve-year-old, I decided to write a letter to the Western Horseman magazine, which had a section where kids asked for pen pals who loved horses. The letter was published, and I received about two hundred fifty letters from other horse-crazed young girls, and a few boys, from around the country. That confirmed I was completely righteous in my passion; there were others out there just like me. *We* were not crazy; everybody *else* was nuts. I still have one of those pen pals as a friend today. Like me, Yvonne is still a horse fanatic. She keeps her Quarter Horse close to where she lives near Los Angeles.

Looking back now, I expect either my parents did not recognize the first signs of an addiction, or they were in denial and hoped it would go away, or they were totally blindsided.

It didn't go away. It only got worse, and that, of course, was for the better, because I was not crazy. Everybody else who didn't love horses was.

Stormy's last racetrack trainer, Chris, had called me up out of the blue and said she'd changed her mind; she didn't want to run him this year after all, and she'd sell him to me, for a thousand dollars. I couldn't have been more gobsmacked or thrilled if I'd won the lottery. I still didn't have a truck or trailer or land or home, but there was never a question, never a hesitation. I would put him in my bedroom if I had to.

"YES!" I screamed in the phone. "YES!"

It had taken a couple of months to get Stormy transported from Washington to Bridgeport, California, where I worked for the Forest Service, and I'd gotten permission to board him with the Forest Service herd.

That is, the District Ranger had given me permission to put Stormy with the herd. The Forest Service horses had not okayed it.

Stormy was shunned. The horses were mean to him. He fit nowhere in the close-knit herd, the exclusive group that had been together for years and had their hierarchies firmly worked out. There wasn't even a lowly slot for Stormy at the very bottom of the totem pole.

I was racked with guilt, watching him stand alone, his herd instinct forcing him to try working his way closer to the group, and being driven away with teeth and hooves, again and again, if he got any closer to them than that fifty-foot invisible barrier. I felt awful when he lifted his head high in the air for me to scratch the terribly itchy bug-bite welts on his neck, and I winced when I fingered the outline of teeth marks and missing hair in his hide; punishment for wanting a friendship.

But horses sometimes knew more than we did. When Stormy saw me and nickered at me, when he stood there and let me hug his neck and bury my face in his mane, he was telling me that it was all going to be okay one day, because we were meant to be together.

It only took thirty-seven years, but I owned a horse, and not just any horse, but Stormy, The Most Beautiful Horse On The Planet.

Chapter 10—California

CRASH

SOME DAYS YOU JUST WANT TO SIT DOWN, PUT YOUR HEAD IN YOUR HANDS, AND CRY.

CRICKET, 1998

The concept of it is so idyllic: saddling up and loading the pack string, settling down the cowboy hat and buckling on the brush-worn chaps, putting your scuffed boot into the stirrup and mounting up, and leading your string of horses down the trail through the forest into the pristine wilderness for a couple of days of quiet enjoyment.

But there can be other perspectives to packing besides bucolic recreation. Things like being caught in a thunderstorm on high ground with a whole string. Or times of equipment malfunctions, like when your mule's saddle pad slips out from under the saddle, *every damn two hours,* and you must stop the string, tie them to trees, unload the heavy loads from the tall mule, unsaddle, adjust the pad, re-saddle, throw the heavy loads back on the pack saddle of the tall mule and tie them down, untie the horses from the trees and back into a line before getting started on the trail again; stop in two hours and repeat. Or days when you get chilled in a snowstorm and stay frozen all day, while hoping your horses can find the trail out of the wilderness when it's buried under two feet of fresh overnight snow because you forgot your map. Or when you watch your whole pack string run off down the trail in the backcountry without you, carrying your map and all your supplies while you stand on foot watching them, without knowing if you will ever see them again. Or when your horse's load slips to one side, he freaks, breaks out of the pack string, flips over backward, and falls down a cliff.

When it came down to it, I discovered the reality that there is nothing remotely romantic or relaxing, or particularly fun, about horse packing, unless you have one of those very rare-as-a-blue-diamond lucky stress-free days where nothing goes wrong. I think I had one of those in all my years as a packer.

But I still chose to do it, and in an indirect way, the challenge of horse packing helped save my soul.

A veterinarian friend at the racetrack had seen the dying coals in my eyes that had replaced the spark of enjoyment I used to have. "Why don't you work for the Forest Service?" he had asked. "I was a fire lookout for a couple of summers when I was younger."

The Forest Service. Outdoors. Forests. Mountains. Scenic beauty. Physical work. No more worrying about racehorses. No more seeing Stormy in another barn. A good place to escape to and forget.

I looked up the Forest Service in the blue pages—it was back in those days when we still relied on phone books. (The Dark Ages before the Internet Saved The World.) There was the phone number for the U.S. Department of Agriculture jobs. I called it. It was a recording, made so easy to use. The menu offered me my choice of job openings in my choice of states. I naturally chose every state in the West, and every outdoor job for which to apply.

I soon got phone calls, from various Forest Service employers in the Western states. I got rather excited about the call from Mark in Bridgeport, a small, picturesque town nestled against the eastern slopes of the Sierra Nevada Mountains in California. "Trail crew," he said, in summary. "Hard work. Hiking. Horses pack in our supplies. Six months. Starts in May."

I said yes. I fled the racetrack. I fled Stormy. I fled a lost dream and a broken heart. I threw myself into my new career as a trail crew worker for the Forest Service.

A perk of working on the Humboldt-Toiyabe trail crew based out of Bridgeport, besides the other bonuses of being outdoors most of the time, hiking, camping, working hard in the mountains and forests, and learning to build trails and rock structures by hand, was that it took a pack string of horses to get our work gear into the wilderness. And from the beginning, I was the lucky one, the only one on my trail crew, who worked regularly with horses. I always jumped at the chance to help with and learn all aspects of the packing, from catching and transporting the horses, packing the loads evenly, saddling the horses and loading the panniers and gear, and tying on a mantie, or tarp, with a diamond hitch. I even got to ride a horse and lead part of the pack string a couple of times with one of the Forest Service Rangers.

Packing was an art, one you only learned by doing, and doing a lot. And the more you did it, the more you realized you didn't really know. Horses were big animals. Sometimes unpredictable. Heavy if they landed on you. Perhaps deadly. One horse could spook, slip, fall, bolt, slip a load—you name it. Eight horses in a string could do this eight-fold, if things really went sideways. One Ranger had a packhorse flip over and get wedged upside down between rocks, and when she tried to extricate him, she was kicked badly enough in the forehead she had to be choppered out.

We had the best packhorses in the world, but . . . they were still horses and a mule. I developed a kind of love-hate relationship with horse packing. I coveted the extra job helping with the packing, and I loved leading a pack string with a Ranger, as it made me feel essential, and *important*. But . . . there was always that nagging stress, the knowledge that something could and sometimes did go dreadfully wrong, way out in the wilderness, that always tainted any yearning I might have had to be a full time horse packer.

The Forest Service horses spent most of their non-working time in the Sierra foothills where I roomed and boarded on my days off. I hiked out to visit them, I hung out with them, I spoiled them with carrots. I could take them out and ride them whenever I wanted, and that was encouraged, to get them into shape for their working summers. I even got paid extra for doing it, though I would have ridden them anyway, because it only reinforced my acquaintance and bond with them, which strengthened our working relationship.

I got to know some horse packers at Leavitt Meadows Pack Station, from where my trail crew sometimes headed into the wilderness. That's where I met Cricket and learned about the crying thing. So far, I'd only ridden in a thunderstorm or two (which was scary enough for me), so I didn't understand quite what he meant yet, though I was capable of imagining quite a few death-like scenarios by myself without any prompting. Things usually went fairly smoothly when I assisted a Ranger with the packing, where that person carried most of the responsibility. I did learn to always pack along my sense of humor and my patience, to leave my watch at home, and to always ride with a buck knife on my belt.

And I learned right away that if you had a choice, choose to work with the best packhorses in the world: horses like our Missouri Foxtrotters Paiute, Tom, Zak, Chino, JD, and Redtop, and a mule like Brenda. They'd worked together on my Forest Service district for at least four years before I arrived. They were unbelievably strong, stout, trail-wise, and downright sensible. They were patient and forgiving; the best horses to teach a greenhorn packer the art of packing.

But, they were horses, and some days, I just wanted to sit down, put my head in my hands, and cry.

A faint tinge of fall whispered on the Sierra breeze as Ranger Margaret and I rode up the trail to Crown Lake in the Hoover Wilderness, leading the pack string carrying food and gear for my trail crew's ten-day work tour. It was sixteen miles round trip, and we had climbed halfway to our campsite. We'd gotten an early start and were making good time.

Margaret rode Tom, leading three loaded horses ahead of me: Paiute, Zak, and Chino. I followed on my horse Stormy, leading a loaded Redtop. Each packhorse carried around 150-pound loads, divided evenly into the panniers hanging off both sides of their packsaddles. Some of them carried top loads too. When we used Brenda the mule, she always carried the tools in her panniers, and the big propane tank that we used for our cooking stove, tied securely on top of her saddle's crossbucks. We occasionally joked about hoping Brenda wouldn't slip and fall down or drop her propane tank along the way. So far she hadn't—mules are known for their sure-footedness.

Our trail passed scenic Barney Lake, with Kettle Peak and the Nugget reflected sharply in the still waters. Above Barney Lake, the horses splashed through Robinson Creek, and followed the narrow, twisting trail, over rock steps that my trail crew had rebuilt the year before, that climbed alongside and above the steeply tumbling waters.

Our horses had been on this trail dozens of times over the years. They could have done it in their sleep. It was around one of these sharp twists in the trail that Zak's load shifted suddenly. He froze. Tied in the middle of the string, Zak's lead rope, which was tied to Paiute's neck, yanked him forward. Behind him, Chino had stopped. That tightened Chino's lead rope, which was tied around Zak's neck, which yanked Zak backwards. That caused Zak's load of ice chests to flip completely underneath his belly, and Zak jerked back in abrupt panic.

What happened next right in front of me and Stormy unraveled in slow motion, but I sat petrified in my saddle, my mouth hanging open, and I couldn't react; all my sensibilities were frozen in shock.

Margaret had the sense to immediately bail off Tom with her buck knife in hand, running for Zak's lead rope, hoping to cut him free. She slashed his front rope, and she quickly leaped to Chino's head to cut his lead rope—she sliced it but it was too late. Panicked by the rough jerking and his load flipping, Zak reared in the air, but with no ropes anchoring him to Paiute anymore, nothing to pull him down, he went straight over backwards—and over the cliff.

WHOOMP he landed on his back, thirteen hundred pounds of flopping horseflesh and the ice chests smashing into the ground, flipping over his nose backwards into the slope of willows. *WHOOMP* down the cliff, out of sight. *WHOOMP* the brush closing up behind him and swallowing all knowledge of a blond horse that had passed that way—and now the terrifying finality of absolute silence.

We killed Zak.

Margaret started screaming. The rest of the horses began neighing in nervousness. I came to and found myself standing on the ground in front of Margaret, grabbing her by the shoulders and shaking her hard, yelling, "IT'S ALL RIGHT! *IT'S ALL RIGHT!*" and she stopped screaming—though we both knew it wasn't all right. We stood paralyzed for a moment longer, shock carving our faces into utter anguish.

We killed Zak.

Some of the horses started wandering on up the trail; that snapped us back to real time. We grabbed the loose horses and tied them to trees, and then we plunged down the steep, muddy hillside of thick willows, slipping, falling, following the crash path of Zak.

Adrenaline now rocketed through my system, doubling the shaking that had begun in my muscles.

"Dead, *dead,*" the voice chanted in my head, I knew we were going to find Zak dead, neck broken.

But nothing prepared me for what I saw.

Not only was Zak alive, but he was *standing in the creek.* He had landed in the only flat spot in that whole creek, a little horse-sized cubbyhole one horse-length square, and horse-chest-deep. If he'd fallen five feet further upstream, he'd have hit waterfall cliffs that would have smashed him to pieces and he would have fallen dead into this hole. If he'd fallen five feet further downstream, he'd have fallen another twenty sheer feet off a waterfall cliff that would have killed him instantly. The Horse Gods were watching out for Zak.

Zak stood in this waterhole, load-less, trembling, in shock, staring at us, panic just below the surface of the shock.

"Zak, Zak . . ." I murmured softly, slipping into the water with him, grabbing his halter. I stroked his face and kept talking to him in a soothing voice; he looked up the cliff with widening eyes to where his buddies still sent out an occasional "Hey, Zak, you okay?" whinny.

Zak wanted out of this water hole and back up on the trail with the safety of the herd. The only way out he saw was *nowhere*, and a wildness started to surface in his eyes, and his body started to gather as if for a big lunge. There was nowhere to leap but forward, and forward was death. I cradled his head, hard. I talked to him, pleaded with him, "Don't move, *please*, don't move, Zak."

Margaret had climbed back up the steep slope to fetch a lead rope, pulling herself up by grabbing onto the willows. We had no radio with us—a big slip-up—so we were on our own here.

I could not believe it, but, as I dared to let go of his head and run my hands down Zak's sides, and down his legs, submerging to my neck in the frigid water, it appeared that *nothing was broken* on Zak. In fact, the only hurt I could find was a cut on his lower lip that was steadily dripping blood into the creek.

Margaret fell and slid back down the cliff to us with a long lead rope. I stayed at Zak's head, as Margaret eased into the small pool, and with her knife, she cut the packsaddle's cinch and threw the saddle and pad aside. Cans and boxes of food bobbed in the pool like apples in a barrel. One of us stayed at Zak's head while the other moved carefully, pulling the floating ice chests, panniers, and food items out of the way.

We looked up for a way out—and there was just nowhere to go. The other side of the creek was a sheer rock face going straight up. In front of and below us was the twenty-foot drop to death. The only possible way out was climbing up, the way Zak had fallen down . . . and that was impossible. But it was also impossible that he was standing there, alive.

Some days you just want to sit down, put your head in your hands, and cry. Now, I got it. I really knew what that old packer had meant.

Zak was calmer now with both of us girls beside him, moving and talking quietly and calmly, but when Zak heard more neighs from above, he whinnied back to them, rolled his eyes, and again gathered for a leap. "No, Zak, no, Zak," I pleaded, rubbing his head, telling him he was fine. If he jumped, he was dead. I didn't want to go over the edge with him either.

How on earth were we going to get him out?

I took off my heavy wet chaps, which were dragging me down, and threw them aside. Margaret snapped the lead rope to Zak's halter and held him, rubbing his head and talking to him, while I took a turn climbing up the slope to search for a path—leaping to the first slim foothold by slipping and jumping and scrambling and pulling myself up. Zak could not turn around—in fact, could not shift positions in the pool at all, so he would have to leap several feet straight up out of the water while turning 180 degrees at the same time. I had no idea how he could even do this, but, if he did make it that far, I tried to scout the best way further up through the slick mud and tall willows on the steep slope so he could keep going from there.

It would be a blind scrabble for all of us—no way to see our footing, no way to see if we would land in a hole, on boulders, rocks, downed logs, tree stumps—Zak had just missed smashing into a tree stump on the fall down—or slick mud that would snatch our footing away and slide Zak right back down in the creek, or on down the death-fall over the waterfall cliff.

From above, I shook my head in despair at Margaret. It wasn't going to work. There was no way we were going to get this horse back up the cliff. I had visions of him having to be shot . . . but we were at least half a dozen hours away from even a bullet. Zak would not stand in that one spot in the creek for six hours.

I slid back down into the creek, frustrated, angry tears leaking from my eyes. "It's impossible!"

"Let's just try," she said. "Maybe *he'll* find a way."

Margaret took the end of the long lead rope, and crawled up the slope several feet above, to where Zak would be facing her if he managed to jump to the first foothold.

She then called Zak's name, and put pressure on his lead rope. I stood at the edge of the pool on the far side of him, pushing on Zak's shoulder, indicating the way to go—though to him it must have looked like an impossible leap to nowhere.

Zak balked. His instinct told him to follow Margaret, but his body wanted to flee, escape by jumping forward—down the waterfall.

"Git up, Zak," I said. I shoved his shoulder, then popped him on the butt with my hand. Margaret pulled on his head, upward and behind him, insistent, but not too hard, because Zak would need his head for this impossible maneuver. I think he understood what we wanted; he just didn't see what he was supposed to do about it.

But Zak wanted out of that water hole. And he trusted us.

He looked at Margaret up and over his shoulder, and started to gather himself, and that amazing horse leaped and turned at the same time for Margaret—scrambling, slipping, almost falling to his nose, miraculously making it up to the little foothold on the slope—at which point he saw a solid wall of impassible willows reaching almost vertically above him, so he neatly leaped a 180-degree turn right back down into his safe water hole in the creek.

"NO!" we yelped.

I jumped back to Zak's head and held him to calm him back down, as he stood there shaking. We three stood there a moment, gathering our willpower and courage. He had to do it. He *had* to do it, or he was a dead horse. There was no other choice. He was afraid, but Margaret and I were determined now, because if we weren't, we would be scared too and there would be nothing left to do but cry.

I broke off a willow branch for a whip. Margaret scrambled higher into the willows, holding onto the very end of the lead rope, hoping Zak would make the same leap again, but this time keep scrambling upwards toward her.

Margaret pulled on his lead rope again.

I said, "Git up, Zak!" and popped him on the butt, and when he didn't move, I hollered, "GIT UP, ZAK!" and whipped his butt hard, as Margaret gave a hard yank on his rope.

Zak leaped up and turned in mid-air again, stumbling and slipping, grasping for the single foothold again, and before he could think I jumped up right after him, reaching up to slash him hard on the butt again with the willow branch. "GET UP!" I screamed, and Margaret pulled with all her might.

This was it. Either Zak made it up this time, or we were done, there would be no other shot. If he jumped back down into the water hole, he wouldn't try this again. I whipped his butt again, willing his upward motion. Zak didn't hesitate but continued clawing and slipping his way upward blindly through the solid wall of rock and willows, though he could not see nor feel a way up the cliff. But he was committed now, and he followed the upward pull on his head toward Margaret, and responded to the whip from behind, and followed that internal herd instinct that also pulled him upward toward his companions and safety.

"GIT UP!" I bellowed, lashing Zak from behind. Margaret yanked desperately on the lead rope, as Zak slipped and spun his wheels in the mud. He went down to his belly, and started sliding backwards. He floundered back to his feet; he lunged and slipped and fell again. He leaped blindly—by sheer luck not landing in any holes, on logs, or tripping over the tangled willow branches. I slipped and fell, but I struggled back up and kept whipping his butt. If he gave up now, we would not get him up this slope again.

Zak could have, should have, fallen to his nose and slid back down in sheer exhaustion and defeat, but he fought tenaciously. *UP* we roared, *UP* we pulled and lashed, *UP* that blond horse battled, struggling for his life. I slipped and fell down again behind him, watched his hind feet churn madly right above my head; I grabbed onto willows and jerked myself out of the way, but I kept yelling and whipping. Margaret kept pulling, and Zak kept grappling.

Then Margaret lost *her* footing, *and* the lead rope, and she began sliding down, wildly grabbing for willows to keep from sliding into Zak's path.

Zak kept going up.

Somehow, that horse clambered past Margaret, made it up the rest of that cliff with no footing, no path, nothing but the pure instinct of fighting onward—crashing upward blindly, clawing his way back up to survive.

Margaret and I sprawled on the trail, panting. Zak walked up to Redtop and nickered, and life was good again.

We were all three completely unscathed—all except for Zak's lip that still steadily dripped blood—and exhausted.

But now that we were all safe, and in one piece, we still had a long way to go. By now, we should have reached the trail crew camp. Very soon, they were going to realize something must have happened, but, with no radio communications, it would still be at least an hour before anybody reached us here, if they even started back on the trail toward us.

After a brief rest, we made sure all the horses were securely tied, then we set about retrieving what we could of Zak's load—two ice chests and whatever food flotsam we could retrieve from the pool.

We fell and slipped our way back down to the water hole— still marveling that the Horse Gods had plopped Zak into the only spot in that creek that didn't kill him. We piled the wet saddle pad onto the slope with the saddle, and bobbed for cans and jars in the pool. We stuffed what we retrieved into the ice chests, and used the rope to haul the food and tack back up the cliff to the trail.

We'd just finished our last climb down and up the slope with everything we could recover, when Mark showed up. He was quite relieved to see we were all in one piece. It was now late in the afternoon, too late to finish the round trip with the pack string.

Margaret would continue up the trail with the rest of the string and drop off the food and gear that the trail crew was waiting for, and camp overnight with them. I'd turn around now on Stormy and escort Zak back out, and drive them home to the barn. I would come back and pick up Margaret and the rest of the pack string tomorrow. We had no horse drugs with us, and I was afraid Zak might have some internal injuries; and at the least, he might get so stiff overnight that he'd have trouble walking in the morning. He looked fine now, but it was better to take him out now while he could still move all right.

We unloaded a couple of horses, repacked what we could from Zak's load into their ice chests, and reloaded them.

Margaret and Mark headed up the trail to camp with the loaded string, while Stormy and I turned around and headed down the trail, leading Zak. The evening sun had already sunk behind the purple peaks of the Sierras. It had been a beautiful day that morning when we'd started out, and it was a beautiful evening now, but in a different way.

I looked back at the brave blond horse walking behind me, and I leaned forward to rest my hands on Stormy's neck as we rode along, thankful we were all fine, and that I could, after all, count this pack trip as another successful one. If you looked at it that way, it was a good day because we didn't have to sit down and cry at the end of it.

Stormy the former racehorse was the perfect escort for a wounded comrade, serenely leading an unruffled Zak out of the wilderness under a bright moon—just another day in the life of a couple of packhorses.

Chapter 11—Texas

SHATTERED II

It is a leisurely ride with endurance friends on a beautiful winter day on appealing trails.

Then—pandemonium.

Ducks fly up from a pond. Horses spook and jump and spin and a sudden explosion fractures the scene, the sound of a mighty *CRACK!* and a violent whirling and the universe is brutally turned on its head.

The *CRACK!* fills my head. The *CRACK! is* my head, my bones, my face shattering into a hundred pieces.

The violent whirling *is* my head, my whole body, orbiting a backwards flip in the air, launched by a shod hind hoof of a temporarily duck-startled and panicked horse.

As I spin above the ground, time passes in split seconds, but in another sphere, it is minutes, or hours. A debate is taking place there.

"Will she live or will she die?"

It is discussed amongst them. I am not a part of the decision; I am suspended mid-air and I can only wait for the verdict.

It lasts a while, this parley, though in this world it is a fraction in time. The decision is finalized when I hit the dirt, face first: *She will live.*

And so I live.

Instinctively I push myself up from the ground. I am no longer the same person. Something has gone horribly wrong. I stare dumbly at the ground. My face is frozen. Numb. Huge. I can't swallow. *I can't swallow,* I try to say, but nothing moves. Nothing comes out.

Voices around me. A hand lifts my face upward.

"OH, MY GOD!" and the hand disappears.

My head falls downward again and I look to the dirt. *I can't swallow.*

Someone hands me a glove and presses it on my lower lip; robotically I hold it there. The glove quickly becomes wet. More voices, a flurry of motion and hoof beats. Hands hold my shoulders as I stare transfixed at the black dirt. I can't think beyond, *I have had a very big accident,* but I feel nothing—no fear, no panic, no pain, because my mind has shut everything else out that is not important. I can't swallow, but that is not important. I can breathe and I can see. So I breathe, sitting on the ground looking at the dirt, detached.

Time passes. Two medics are there. My mind forms an image of my sister. *Call your sister.*

"Call my sister," I whisper. Someone writes it down as I painstakingly form each number with a mouth that does not move and a voice that does not work.

The two medics are holding me up. We are a quarter mile from a parking lot. I must be walking between them.

I am lying inside an ambulance and I am holding a suction tube in my mouth. An IV is jabbed into the back of my hand and it hurts like hell. But soon I forget that because I am swiftly being swept into some unfamiliar, unforgiving, unfair universe far beyond the prick of a needle—the bursting of a dam, flooding, growing exponentially, of shocking pain.

I am in a room, lying on a cold hard table with a machine over my head. The technician tells me to roll over one way. The pain is terrible. Roll over the other way. I choke out a cry with every movement.

I am so cold. Pain is excruciating. My eleven-year-old great nephew is beside me, his hand on my forehead because I have begun convulsing.

"Doctor!" My sister's frightened voice cries out.

I am in an ambulance again. Pain . . . *ohmigod—pain*. My great nephew holds the suction tube in my mouth. In and out of consciousness.

I am lying on another hard table, still holding a suction tube in my mouth. It still siphons a steady stream of blood. I must throw up but I don't want to mess up the nice hospital. I roll over in agony and throw up on the floor. Nurse throws a towel on it as she walks by without stopping. I pass out again.

My eyes open to a man in green standing over me. Hands reach down to my face, thumbs crawl in my mouth, and *press down*, feeling the moving parts. The parts that aren't supposed to move.

A sound gradually fills my consciousness, a low, slow, morbid, deliberate, *HA, HA, HA, HA.* It is my chortling, my screams. They spill out my broken mouth as a macabre laugh. *HA, HA, HA, HA, HA.*

"Stop, please stop," I beg him, I try to push him away, but no words actually come out and I have no strength, and nobody will come help me as he keeps prodding, probing indelicately with his hands in my mouth, looking at an X-ray on the wall, feeling the breaks, the grinding pieces of bone, re-tearing my already-gone lower lip, as I weep in moaning laughs, *HA, HA, HA, HA.*

My eyes open. Movement. People. Busy. Noisy. Machines beeping.

No pain. I feel nothing but very weary, very heavy. Emptiness after a lost battle.

My sister, beside my bed, where she has been standing, on her feet for six hours, because they will not give her a chair.

My smiling Raven puppet, sitting on my stomach, where my sister has set it.

I am desperately parched. I am offered a cup of water with a straw but I can't swallow.

Two green-shirted surgeons are at the foot of my bed, proclaiming, "Three breaks, lower jaw. Upper jaw shattered. Pulverized . . . plates . . . screws." Smiling, ". . . good as new."

It doesn't matter. I close my eyes and drift.

My niece kisses me on the forehead. Tears slip from my eyes.

It is night in another room. My sister has gone. My cousins are sitting beside my bed. Nurse hands me something to sign. I understand nothing but suffering. I can't hold a pen. My cousins sign the paper.

Overpowering pain pulls me back back back down into unconsciousness.

I have learned a new language, a dialect of incapacitating, strangling, drowning pain. It has become my unbidden soulmate, my existence. There is no refuge from my soul, no refuge from this other world of unfathomable agony.

There is a clock in my room. It says 11:00. The morphine no longer keeps the crushing pain away. I'm at the bottom of an immense ocean of complex layers of torment. I lay there for hours suffocating, utterly defenseless. Destroyed. I open my eyes. The clock says 11:10. Ten minutes or twelve hours? Morning or night? I have no idea. Does it matter?

I ask for more morphine. When it seeps into my veins, it doesn't lessen the pain as much as it provides company for the pain in the cruel form of fast-flashing, exhausting dreams.

I don't know if I'm going to make it through this. The conscious thought hits me twice during the day, but there's nothing to do about it. And I don't care. I'll either live or die. If I don't make it, it doesn't matter. I don't have any fleeting regrets. I don't think of my family or my horse. I have no other thoughts. I just lie there, and wait for every dragging second to pass into the next unending second, and into the next torturously slow second . . . surrounded, weighted down, choking on incomprehensible pain.

A woman comes in and asks me if I want her to pray for me. I whisper yes. She takes my hand and my sister's, says a prayer for me. She leaves. I go back to caring about nothing and swimming through the murky sea of semi-consciousness, morphine, wild flashing raving dreams and pain, waiting for every second to drag by. I lie for a lifetime in that state.

I am home slowly healing, when six weeks after the accident, a sudden and deep depression devours me. I spend my days sitting in the dark; I cry, and I cry. It does not make sense. Logic tells me I survived, and I will recover completely. I am mostly free from pain; the bones will heal; my lip will grow back; my teeth will be replaced. I should be grateful. I should be happy. I *know* this. But the rationale evades me. It is hard to move out of bed. It is hard to care about eating. I care about nothing, and for days, I can only weep in the dark.

Two weeks later, I crawl out of the depression and back on a horse. Perhaps it shows poor judgment, riding again so soon, when any facial trauma is going to have severe consequences. But I have to do it. I was afraid that I would be scared to ride, and part of my life would be over if I could not ride a horse.

But when I climb aboard this horse, even though my body is not healed, and my brain is saying other things, my soul has not been shattered. Other things have been taken from me, but I am not afraid to ride.

My world has been forever altered by this twist of fate. I'm not the same person I was. But my soul is shaped by horses, and *I am not afraid to ride.*

Chapter 12—California

Zayante
9900 miles. One endurance horse. Four hooves.
60 Top Tens
5 Best Conditions
4 Tevis buckles

Ninety-nine hundred miles. Think about that: it's the distance of more than twice around the United States. It would take an extraordinary horse to accomplish this mileage feat—perhaps a lustrous white Arabian, through whose veins might flow the pure blood of the finely-bred Bedouin horses of the Arabian sands. He would be intelligent and strong, noble and proud. His endurance would be inexhaustible, his heart monstrous. A ride on his sturdy back would be a treasured gift from the Horse Gods.

Shut inside a dark stall in Pomona, California, at the Equine Affaire, a big national annual horse exposition, and peeking out because he was afraid to get close to his door, was an endurance horse with that very mileage and stamina and intelligence, though his appearance was the antithesis of such an accomplished equine. Zayante was scruffy, dirty white, and quite bewildered. It was very possible he had never lived in a stall in his life.

To an endurance horse, this was a bizarre world: here at this Equine Affaire were Bedouin-costumed riders on elegant horses whose glistening tails swept the ground. Round-muscled Quarter Horses wearing western saddles and silver sparkles grandly carried their big-hatted big-belt-buckled cowboy partners. Halter-less horses followed people around like big dogs. There were high-stepping horses whose knees almost smacked their noses at the trot. There were parade horses, champion horses, movie-star horses. Partially blocking Zayante's view of the equine circus was a rolling horse palace with the name Parelli on it, which must have been awfully important because it was so much bigger and fancier than Zayante's own humble dust-covered rattly three-horse trailer.

He had come from a questionable background: snagged by a horse trader named Laddie from the back paddock of a fancy Arabian breeding stable at two for $100 after his original owner skipped out on his board bill. Unbroke and uncut, and ruling his pasture kingdom, the young colt had been known to terrorize the stable girls that were assigned to feed him. Laddie immediately gelded him and shortly traded him to a horse packer named Billy, who broke him to saddle and used him to lead pack strings in the Sierra Nevada Mountains. That packer knew he had a special horse on his hands. He had dreams of riding his beloved gray gelding that he'd named Taco up the entire Pacific Crest Trail to Canada, and back down the Continental Divide; but circumstances dictated that he sell the horse to some acquaintances.

The new owners, the Bumgardners, happened to be endurance riders, and that was where the gelding hit his marvelous stride.

From the Bumgardners, Bob and Julie Suhr bought and rode the gray gelding they christened Zayante for his first five years in endurance; eighty-nine rides and over five thousand miles without a pull. Along the way he finished the tough 100-mile Tevis Cup four times in a row, and had forty-two Top Ten finishes and won five Best Condition awards. Since Zayante could be a bit of a spirited, spooky horse on the trail, and since Bob and Julie were getting to be a little older and didn't like to hit the ground so much, they sent Zayante back to Jackie Bumgardner. Jackie had been riding Zayante ever since, adding another couple thousand miles and over a dozen Top Ten finishes to his resume; and that's when I joined the Zayante

Fan Club. Some of us members tended to fight with each other a bit, over who loved Zayante more and who would get to ride him in the next endurance ride.

It mattered to none of us that Zayante officially had no papers. Despite his dubious background, and underneath the scruff, Zayante was, even to an untrained eye, unmistakably the perfect classic, athletic, purebred Arabian in size and conformation.

We nicknamed him the Energizer Bunny: he kept going, and going. He thrived on multi-day rides, particularly five days in a row of fifty miles a day, looking as good at the end of the last day as he did at the beginning of the first. He was calm at the vet checks, saving his energy, never excited, looking pleasant and interested and polite. He was push button to ride—after all, at twenty-one or so years of age and almost ten thousand endurance miles, Zayante had pretty much seen and done it all. He always knew where he was positioned in regards to the rest of the pack in a ride, and sometimes he thought you were going a little slower than necessary to get the job done. If you didn't listen to him and pick up the pace, he could jig for *fifty miles*. He always knew which way to go, and he wouldn't let you take a wrong turn on a trail. Zayante excelled at endurance and he loved it. You could see it in his eyes; you could feel it when you were on his back. I had never been on a better endurance horse—he was an absolute joy to ride.

Statistically, he was one of the best and highest-mileage endurance horses in the country, and ironically, that was what landed him in this despicable stall in this polluted overcrowded city amongst such strange horses, where he clearly didn't belong. Zayante, and his fellow endurance horse and herd-mate Holly, would be an exhibit in the endurance clinic that Jackie was giving at this Equine Affaire. It was somewhat of an honor, but Zayante couldn't figure out what he had done to land him here in this prison.

I had come along to help Jackie with the horses, being one of Zayante's biggest fans and one of his riders. I'd known Zay for three years, and had ridden him in one hundred and fifty miles of endurance competition, and at least triple that in training miles. We made a good team, Zayante and I, and I thought we made a nice picture of partnership out on the trail. I knew his eccentricities, and he knew my peculiarities—though truthfully, those were few, because

I had become a decent rider thanks to many miles of endurance riding and conditioning.

To a rather bedraggled, wilderness-type desert-rat endurance rider like me, this was also a bizarre atmosphere: the costumed riders, the dressage riders, the important cowboys, the big-name trainers like Parelli, the sparkles, the silver, the polish, the glitter.

To most endurance riders and horses (especially me and Zayante), looks weren't everything. Most endurance riders and horses tended to not focus so much on the refined aspects of being sparklingly clean; we tended to have less time to work on beautification, what with all the riding we did.

That's the excuse I used, anyway. Ten miles down the trail, you were going to be all hot and dusty, so what was the point of getting all gussied up? And after a ride, an endurance horse really liked to get down in the dirt and roll, good and long and hard, grinding that dirt and sand into his coat. It felt so good; why would you want to go and bathe him and make him all unnatural and clean after that nice coating of dirt in the hair that kept the sun from burning and the bugs from biting? What was truly important was how the horse looked going down the trail.

Besides, Jackie and I had been so busy with riding and conditioning horses lately that we hadn't had time for the triviality of grooming. Zayante had no low self-esteem issues on the endurance trails—no matter the tint of the dirt in his coat, or the angle of the kink in his mane, he was simply a gorgeous animal, inside and out. And he knew it.

I wasn't particularly known for my grooming skills anyway, a carryover from my racetrack grooming days, where I'd sometimes send a horse out to the track with straw in his tail (or worse: a poop smudge on his coat). Hence, the straggly braids Zayante still wore in his mane: we'd completed a 50-mile ride three weeks before, and had been too busy since then doing other endurance things to bother untangling his braids. A braided mane kept him cooler when he worked up a sweat on the trails in winter. The weather this time of year in the desert was too cold for baths for hairy horses; so, as all white horse owners know, those dirty spots showed up quite well on Zayante's white coat.

I did take time here in this alien world of pampered equines, to at least unbraid and smooth out Holly's and Zayante's manes, but they still held crinkles and retained their unruly character of competition horses who'd just come off the trail. Being a bay, Holly naturally looked much cleaner, but Zayante was a mess. We sponged the worst dirt spots off his coat, but without a real bath, Zayante would remain a little less than glamorous—not that it bothered any of us who knew he was a super star.

We walk Zayante and Holly around the barn area to work out the stiffness from the long haul to the big city, but that isn't enough. Zayante doesn't enjoy it anyway. To a horse who has covered thousands of miles in the wilds and who has just about seen all the Horse-Eating-Boogey-Monsters out there on the trail, everything here among the big city barns is dreadfully spooky. People wrestle with and drag around huge snakes that spout water. Hiding behind all the outlandish horse trailers are . . . *Things* . . . waiting to pounce on and devour him. Crackling loudspeakers make him jump. All the brushing and combing and blow-drying makes him suspicious.

Holly takes a pleasant interest in everything going on about her—she'd in fact traveled with Parelli's show for a year—but Zayante tries to shrink right into and behind and underneath Holly to get away from it all. He actually prefers hiding in his scary dark stall to facing the alien monsters in this strange place.

What Zayante and Holly really need is a little exercise under saddle. Alas, the only place available is a warm-up ring. Now, despite me being a fine rider and all, I have never taken to the arena. I dislike it because I'm not good at it, and I'm not good at it because I dislike it. In fact, I rather loathe it. I am like Zayante: I crave the trails. The longer the trail, the farther the horizon, the better the ride. Zayante and I have a date next weekend in the 65-mile Twenty Mule Team Endurance Ride, and like Zayante, I itch to get out of this big city and back to the desert to ride, really ride.

Nevertheless, we are stuck here this weekend, so Jackie and I saddle up Zayante. I grab my helmet but don't bother to put on my riding tights. I leave my shorts on because it's very hot, and this will be a few short quick and easy spins around the arena, and nobody will really notice me out there with all the other horses and riders.

We lead Zayante and Holly to the warm-up arena. Jackie holds Holly outside the arena while I mount up.

Here is where my close relationship with Zayante begins: I just think, *Okay, let's go*, and move the reins slightly, and Zayante goes.

Well—normally that happens. Here, Zayante is afraid to walk away from Holly. I have to actually squeeze my legs, flip the reins a bit, then nudge my heels into his belly to convince him to move away from Holly and toward the arena.

A good number of horses and riders are going around, all of whom look much snazzier than we do: fancy and beautiful breeds of all colors and shapes and sizes, talented dressage riders and skilled cowboys, walking and trotting and cantering and spinning and sidepassing, working circles and figure eights. It is all neatly choreographed equine dance in the arena.

The same arena that Zayante does *not* want to enter and exercise.

I take another look at the horses and riders Zayante is dubiously eyeballing. There's been a lot of brushing and polishing and painting happening in the stables of Pomona, on horses and humans. I look down at Zay's disheveled mane—kinky wisps of white hairs sticking up in all directions. It reminds me that I probably did not bring a hairbrush along for myself on this trip. I self-consciously try to stuff a little more hair under my helmet, pull my shorts down a little further, and futilely smooth a particularly noticeable eruption in Zay's mane.

I manage to get Zayante through the gate and into the arena, but he moves directly over to where Holly is hanging over the rail and he plants himself there.

"Good boy," I say, "let's wait for a good opening to melt into the crowd." We watch the stylish riders and horses go around for a while.

Okay, let's get this over with, both of us think—though we seem to be of two minds as to how to accomplish it. I am thinking, *Let's take a few spins around the arena*, and Zay is thinking, *Let's just walk back out and stand by Holly*.

I have to grapple Zayante into the exercising fray, aiming to keep him on the rail, at a walk. He doesn't *want* to walk forward; he moves sideways and slowly. I urge him with my legs, and say, "Come on, Zayante, let's get trotting." His disinclined trot, moving away from Holly, is much the same—dragging, staggering off the rail. Other riders going faster than us (everybody) are having to give us a wide berth because of our erratic path. We ping-pong to the end of the arena, and as we sweep around back in the direction of Holly and Jackie, Zayante springs into a canter, for which I am not quite prepared.

"Easy, Zay," I croon, pulling him back to a trot—a big extended trot. I have a hard time keeping him on the rail because he wants to take the shortest diagonal path across the arena back to Holly.

When we do get back to Holly and Jackie, I assume we are naturally going to keep moving, because in the close horse and rider alliance that we always share, we are of one mind and I have not asked Zayante to stop. Zayante naturally assumes we are finished with exercise for the day, and he slams on his brakes. I pitch forward over his neck.

Settling myself squarely back in the saddle, I ask, then squeeze, then kick Zayante back into motion along the rail again. In disagreement, he puts his head down and bulls his way zigzagging off the rail up the arena, stabbing his feet into the ground to produce a rough trot, as he can do so well when he is crabby. He cuts the corner at the end again, and I pull rather insistently on his right rein, and gouge him with my left heel, to try to keep him on the rail as we are coming back. It's not working—Zayante is definitely accomplishing more of a diagonal across the arena. Had I been asking him for a sidepass, it might have been acceptable, but I did not ask for that, and it does not even qualify as a proper sidepass anyway. This is a true Battle of the Wills.

When we get back to Holly on this round, before he can slow down, I squeeze Zayante hard to keep him moving on past her for another loop. He gives a wretched, pathetic, desperate, "Holly, I need you!" whinny.

I have noticed that the arena suddenly has many fewer riders.

Possibly this is coincidental.

Zayante bulldozes his way drunkenly to the far end, and, around the corner, he bounds into a canter again. I haul him back, and ask him to trot. He shakes his head and crab-steps to the left, even as I am now starting to crank his head right and use an iron leg on his left side to keep him on the rail. Zay is getting madder and madder at this bogus nonsense and is now twisting his head sideways and grinding his teeth.

This is *not* a good sign.

Normally Zayante has a fearsome sneer that he uses to intimidate other horses on the endurance trail—ears pinned flat against his neck, lips peeled back in a terrific horse grimace. He is using this now, sneering at every horse he passes near. It does not befit his looks as the endurance champion that he is, and it certainly does not overawe any equine left in the arena, or, for that matter, any other human. He just looks crazed.

As we approach Holly again, it feels as if Zayante has tossed out his anchor, which is dragging his grubby white butt to a halt in port.

"Come on, Zay!" I say, and kick him hard past Holly again, up the rail. This time he furnishes a bellow of ire.

At the other end of the arena, the battle is *on*. Zayante bucks. Zayante *never* bucks! Until he is mad enough to get me, his pal, his perfect and skilled riding partner, off his back, because he hates this misrepresentation of exercise on this farce of a trail in this sham of a horse bed and breakfast. He's had ENOUGH.

I fly up onto Zayante's neck from the buck, and as he lunges forward into an infuriated canter, I am thrown backwards onto his back, almost out of the saddle. He lunges left across the arena as I haul on his reins to the right.

I have now become painfully aware that there is only one other horse and rider in the arena. Perhaps this is still coincidental, but I think not. Zayante—or maybe me and my acrobatic style of riding—has sufficiently scared, or more like irritated, everybody out of the arena with the exception of one pair.

Miraculously, they seem to have not noticed us at all. The immaculately, yet not ostentatiously, groomed chestnut Quarter Horse mare, with precisely trimmed mane and gleaming tail, seems to float over the arena with ethereal lightness. And, oh my stars, that cowboy! The mortal wearing the polished boots and silver belt buckle and black cowboy hat—though nothing flamboyant—emanates allure. Sharp blue eyes are set in a face creased with what must possess great character and a great smile (which I am not seeing, only imagining). The shining silver-accented saddle and bridle strikingly set off the mare's golden-red radiance.

Even in my wholly occupied state of trying to stay in the saddle and control my obnoxious horse, I can see perfection at a glance: in the horse's carriage (obviously a champion), and in the rider's faultless seat (obviously a champion). I can see art: the invisible commands and responses, the perfect collected canter, the ultimate human and equine ballet, the mental bond, poetry in perfection, the precise communication, concentration, and partnership between this striking man and stunning mare.

Everything Zayante and I are *not*.

Meanwhile, the raggedy white bull in the china shop, with his grimy black biothane bridle that hasn't been scrubbed in a couple of rides, and his untamed mane and angrily pinned ears, unwillingly carrying his tousled and increasingly disconcerted shorts-clad rider, is still pursuing his goal of leaping and lunging toward Holly and the arena exit. It can safely be said that I have now become a spectacle.

I should just give up and slink from the arena with my tail between my legs in shame, I think, but now it's a matter of principle. I *can* ride, and I *will* ride this bloody horse. I have to prove I can elegantly control my partner, too, like The Cowboy.

Zayante screeches to a stop in front of Holly.

"TROT, damn you!" I hiss, and give Zayante a boot in the side, and Zayante indignantly bolts again into a canter and I almost flip off over his back.

Now I'm mad. I kick Zay up the rail again away from Holly.

Now Zayante is *really* mad too. He bellows his discontent again like a heifer being branded, and jars his feet into the ground in a head-splitting (mine) trot. As we near the far end of the arena, the steering and brakes go completely out. Zayante zooms in a cutting-horse circle back in the direction of Holly, and I have to grab my saddle pommel to keep my seat. I crank Zay's head ninety degrees to the right, and kick hard with my left leg to get him back to the general area of the rail. I would have settled for the rail's zip code.

Meanwhile, despite the scuffling rodeo going on behind them, this impeccable cowboy and horse combination in front of us at the other end of the arena are still perfectly performing the consummate collected canter in flawless figure eights. However, it is quite apparent that they have indeed noticed us and are starting to get a little irritated.

Zayante is oblivious to all but his single purpose of getting back to Holly and out of this godforsaken arena. The enraged white bull I am riding throws his head down and gives a buck again as he lurches into a canter diagonally across the arena straight toward Holly and Jackie. I have now abandoned all attempt at looking like a competent rider, and am now standing in my stirrups, sawing on the reins, horsemanship and partnership out the window, trying to slow my horse down, or steer him back to the rail, one or the other, *anything,* but this is not working at all, and now Zayante is aiming straight for the faultlessly cantering chestnut mare, who is now definitely pinning her ears, because, being in perfect partnership with her perfect rider, she feels her rider's definite exasperation.

As Zayante nears the perfect pair, I realize, to my horror, Zayante is *deliberately moving so as to sideswipe them.* It's his scheme to get us both thrown out of the Equine Affaire. Red-faced, appalled, I seesaw desperately on the reins, steering like a kamikaze, praying for a miracle as we bear down on the Perfect Pair.

Somehow we do not collide, and as we roar closely past Perfection, close enough for them to feel our breeze, Zayante rudely gives the lovely mare one of his most unloveliest sneers and throws in another buck, which pitches me forward again. Even as I shove myself back into the saddle seat, and even though I know what I will get, I cannot help but look at The Cowboy; I cannot help but look into his mesmerizing blue eyes.

And it is not humor I see in the divine eyes of that cowboy. It is not camaraderie, nor is it amusement. It is the dreaded stink-eye.

I land on Zayante's neck again when he skids to a stop right in front of Holly, and then I come back for a landing in the saddle. Zay firmly plants roots into the ground and is finished, period. But that is all right with me, because I have had quite enough of this complete humiliation.

I slither off an unrepentant champion endurance horse, and slink out of the arena in my shorts and deflated ego, still feeling the glares boring a hole in the back of my shorts, still hearing the perfectly synchronized uninterrupted three-beat metronomic clip-clip-clip of perfect cantering hooves carrying a perfectly balanced rider through a now-undisturbed perfect warm-up ride in the arena.

As we switch the saddle to Holly for Jackie to ride, I hold Zayante outside of the arena. He is much happier with that—still in the bleak barn area of this stupid place, but at least he's not being "tortured" in an arena. Zay hangs his head over my neck, because he's my buddy and we desert hicks are both stuck here in this mess together. I reach back and hang my arm over his neck, because we are indeed good pals. Neither of us can hold a grudge.

As Holly performs nicely for Jackie (a good rider), in the arena, the charismatic cowboy finishes his warm-up on his superb little mare. I want to duck my head as the duo rides out of the arena; I want to shrink into the earth (Really, I can ride better than that!), but I cannot help but look up at the man as he passes by us. His eyes—and his mare's—never fall anywhere near us.

I hear people greet the duo: "Hi, Ted." "How are ya, Ted." "She looks good, Ted."

Ted Robinson
7-time NRCHA World Champion
2 Time World's Greatest Horseman: "One rider—One horse—One bit"
All-time leading money earner of the NRCHA
6-Time Snaffle Bit Futurity Winner

Katie Starlight
2 Time World's Greatest Horseman's mount
(with Ted Robinson)

Chapter 13—Egypt

HONEY IN THE DESERT

I longed to gallop in the desert, among the pyramids.

It was another one of those inexplicable desires (like galloping racehorses or Riding Out on an Irish racehorse) that I didn't stop to reason out. While I was getting comfortable riding many different horses for many, many miles thanks to endurance riding, I mostly rode at a trot. Maybe a canter now and then. I still wasn't comfortable reaching a full gallop on a horse—I hadn't purposely done it since that wild ride in Africa nine years earlier, and my Irish racehorses a year before that—but some atavistic fantasy of galloping by the ancient Egyptian relics devoured my thoughts while in Egypt, and I had no reason to question the validity of it. I just had to do it.

I'd traveled to Egypt with endurance friends Jackie, Steph, and Tracy, to assist them in helping a friend, Maryanne, put on a fun endurance ride for the local riding club. While I photographed and took notes for stories, I'd watched with great jealousy as the riders struck out across the desert on a 30-mile ride, and I'd ached for my own four-legged steed to ride beside Abu Sir and Saqqara, beneath the shadow of the Melted Pyramid, around the Bent and the Red Pyramids. *Why not me?* I opined. (Some might say "whined", but I don't whine. Do I?)

In our marvelous two weeks in Egypt, Maryanne had taken us to tour the main sights: the Great Pyramid of Giza (the oldest of the Seven Wonders of the Ancient World), and the sprawling Khan al

Khalili market (where someone offered to trade Maryanne one hundred camels for me); and she'd escorted us on rides through the countryside on some of her excellently trained horses. I'd been to Sharm el Sheikh on the Red Sea, and I'd climbed Mt. Sinai in the stunningly beautiful Sinai Desert, something I never imagined I'd be able to do in a part of the world I'd long fantasized about visiting but never thought practicable.

But despite all the great experiences, I desperately craved that desert gallop. Maryanne's friend Morad had promised to take me out riding in the desert. A regular group went out in the desert every Saturday, and I'd missed the last weekend ride. This Saturday was my last day in Egypt. I'd begged Morad a few days earlier, with my flight-home time clock ticking.

"Remember, I want to ride with you or Paul in the desert on a fast ride! Not far, but just a little gallop in the desert. Not on a scary horse. Oh, and nothing that bucks."

"Oh," Morad had grinned, "I have something special planned for you!"

"What?"

His eyes twinkled, but he wouldn't say any more.

And on my last day in Egypt, Morad had that "special surprise" horse for me to ride. I was beyond thrilled.

Until I saw my horse.

A groom leads out into the sunshine my mount: a large, magnificent flaming red stallion with a flowing mane and white-rimmed eye. Fire steams from his nose. Flames combust from his bulging veins. He tries to savage the groom holding his reins. Nervous, heart crashing cymbals in my ears, I creep hesitantly up to my horse, and the groom hands me the reins and legs me up. The stallion turns his head and tries to bite my leg.

Several times.

The groom lets go, and even with my tight grip on the reins, the horse ducks his head and lifts me out of my saddle (an English saddle, which I am not used to!), and lunges, mouth wide open, at the piddling palm branch we walk under, as if he could devour the whole palm tree in one derisive bite.

As he walks he swaggers, bowing his beautiful head to his chest. His mane ripples over both sides of his neck and his forelock covers his face. His steps are light but he is so terrifically powerful I am like a mosquito on his back.

I notice the reins are extra double duty thick—probably because he pulls so hard he's broken a few. Great! As we walk a short distance down the paved road, he shakes his mighty head and jerks it down again, and I know he could launch me to the moon if he wished.

Oh, Morad, what have you done to me! I throw Morad a tremulous look. He is grinning from ear to ear. "His name is Harry!"

Good to know—I may die on a stallion named Harry today.

We walk down the busy canal road with the group, but my stallion's walk is more an arrogant sashay, as he defiantly throws his butt out into the always-crazy traffic. He prances, roots his head, dances on the cement. I pray he lets me keep my seat on his back as he shows off for everybody. I don't want to fall off and hit the pavement, or get tossed in front of a speeding vehicle.

We turn into the mango grove, which drops us right onto the desert at Abu Ghorab, the ancient Sun Temple. Harry is now walking calmly, but like a stalking cat. I can just feel his taut muscles ready to explode beneath me. Vivid, unwanted memories of Fred, the first racehorse I rode, come rushing back to me, almost knocking me out of the saddle. I remember the feeling of him running away with me, the helplessness, the weakness in my body, *and the fear.*

The pit of my stomach is churning, and I am scared now, as Harry creeps softly over the desert sand, stalking only God knew what.

There are eight of us riding out into the desert. *Oh God,* I think, *we're all going to take off like a cavalry charge, or Morad's going to come racing by me, and Harry's going to deposit me neatly in the sand before we ever get started (thank God it's sand).*

But everybody just walks on, chatting, in no hurry. Morad trots near me, and I say apprehensively, "Morad, um, you might've put me on too much horse . . ."

He just gives me another big smile and says, "He's the lightest one I have," over his shoulder as he canters off to some other riders on a hill. *His lightest one?* Right. I can feel Mount Vesuvius about to blow beneath me and spew me off the top.

Visions of getting my face smashed again jolt into my head, and I cannot stop them. I cannot stop the fear that I am going to get hurt again. *How easy is it to get to a good hospital in Egypt? I wanted to gallop in the desert? What was wrong with me? Why couldn't Morad have just put me on a quiet little gelding instead of this colossal dragon?*

Harry has not actually done anything at all dangerous yet, but I seriously consider turning around, getting off, and walking back home. It won't be the first time I've chickened out on something I'd dreamed of doing.

Morad comes cantering back to our group, and then he and Paul take off galloping up a little hill. Hortense says to me, "Come, we can follow them."

I think: *Well, if Harry bolts off at a dead run, at least he'll be going uphill so it won't be so fast, and it's sand so it won't hurt so much when I plow into it face-first.*

I take a cross with the reins on Harry's neck if I need it to brace against his pull, though so far out here on the sand, I haven't touched his mouth. I am ready though; I know it is coming, sooner or later.

I move my hands just a little, and think *Forward, (but please not too fast!);* and Harry bows his head and floats into a gentle trot. I can feel every powerful bone and muscle and sinew of this horse flowing beneath me. I wanted to gallop in the desert? Heck, this trot is pretty darn nice, fast enough for me.

At the top of the hill where it flattens out, with a view of other cantering horses ahead of us, I think, *Oh dear, here we go . . .* and Harry does nothing but continues floating over the sand at the trot awaiting my next command. I am still barely touching his mouth; the reins are slack. Harry has a big smooth trot and is ahead of Hortense; so she moves Maximus to a canter to catch up with us.

Okay, this *is where Harry bolts away,* I think, *and what the heck, it's time to find out if I'm going to hit the sand or not.* I grit my teeth, I touch my legs to his sides ever so lightly—and Harry bows his flaming head, touches his nose to his chest, and breaks into a canter the same speed as his trot, and I still have never touched his mouth.

Oh my God, I think, *what is this thing I am riding!* Realization starts to dawn on me that this horse Morad has given me to ride may indeed be something special. We continue moving onward, cantering, my fear starting to crumble like the ancient pyramids and settle into dust in the hoof prints we leave in our wake.

We canter up to a group of people, and Paul says to me, "Come with us. Let's go!" and he takes off at a canter.

I say softly to Harry, "Let's go!"

Harry tucks his nose to his chest, and picks up the right lead I ask for. We canter smoothly through the sand, past the pyramids of Abu Sir, erupting as three modest disintegrating triangular mounds out of the sand.

Coming to the top of the little wadi, the desert flattens out— acres and miles and countries ahead of us to ride through. I can ride from here straight to Morocco if I want to—Morocco!

The group canters onward; my wonderful mount and I canter by ourselves thirty yards apart. Much of the footing out here is not as deep as you'd think—a galloping hoof leaves an impression as deep as on a groomed racetrack. Some of the sand is rocky; it almost sounds like hooves on cobblestones. The consistency of the sand changes: from the harder sand to the rocky sand with firmer footing, to soft sand where the hooves do sink down. I can feel the change in the footing and the adjustment in Harry's stride though he never bobbles. I could drink a glass of champagne from his back at a canter and not spill a drop. And I *still* haven't touched his mouth—the reins just rest loosely against his neck.

Harry and I drift further from the pack, in our own little world; and without thinking I have urged him to a gallop. My magnificent red stallion and I flatten out into a gallop, a full out run in the Western Desert, beneath the pyramid and temple complex of Saqqara, when it hits me: *Oh, my God, I am galloping a horse in Egypt by the pyramids! I am in Egypt, galloping by pyramids, and I am not afraid.* I feel I could cry.

I do cry, many times that morning. I never imagined I could do this without fear. And I have never ridden such a horse as this. Harry is so willing. He does everything I ask, as if he is a part of my mind, as if he knows my past fears, as if he knows my hidden strengths I am not yet familiar with myself.

We veer back toward the others, still at a gallop; we climb another hill and our group stops on top to look around us. It is a beautiful partly cloudy and cool day with a slight breeze—just perfect. Pyramids to the north. Pyramids to the south. Unknown buried temples and tombs and ancient mysteries beneath our hooves.

We walk and slide down the steep sand hill, and Paul says, "Let's do the Back Forty," or something like that, and we all take off cantering again. After a half mile, Paul and I fall behind the others, and slow down to a walk to give our horses a breather.

Paul can see how smitten I am with Harry. "He has another name," Paul says. "Asal. It means 'Honey.'"

Harry's previous owner, a British gal, couldn't quite pronounce the Arabic word Asal. "It sounds like Asshole," she'd said, "I'm giving him a new name! He's Harry!"

By now we've lost the others—here riders quickly become spots on the horizon—they'd swung east around a string of sand hills, and we are by ourselves, alone in this great desert. As we walk along talking, I can't keep my hands off Harry. I stroke his beautiful neck, I run my hands through his mane, I pat his big red butt. No queen had ever had a more beautiful seat on a golden throne than I have right here.

"How do you say 'You are beautiful' in Arabic?" I ask Paul.

"'Enta gameel,'" he says. "It means not only physical beauty, but beautiful from the inside."

Oh, *yes*. I lean over Harry and put my arms around his neck and I hug him. "Enta gameel, Asal," I whisper in his ears. My red horse flexes his neck as if he understands me, acknowledging my affection.

We walk until we get out of the deeper sand, and Paul says, "Let's see if we can find them."

Paul moves his horse to a trot, then to a canter. Harry graciously dips his nose and floats into a trot, and nods his head again and glides to a canter. Paul is now galloping, full out, running ahead of us. Harry wants to follow, but he asks me—*asks me!*—if he can go.

"Meshe, Harry!" I holler. Go on!

He benevolently shares his gift of flight with me, spreading his vermillion wings, and we soar through the desert of Egypt. The wind roars in my ears and whips Harry's beautiful mane in my face and drives the tears out of my eyes and across my face. If I cock my head to the side just so, I no longer hear the wind but only the four-beat of his hooves on the ancient sand, throbbing in time with my heart. I drop the reins and put my hands on that golden red neck as he races along, sharing his fearlessness with me. I feel his goodness and strength through my fingertips.

"Enta gameel, Asal!"

The wind dries my tears, and Harry and I slow down. We catch up with Paul who shakes his head laughing at me.

"Let's go that way," he says, pointing. "I'll show you something."

We trot down one hill and cross a little wadi and trot back up another hill. Harry adjusts his strides perfectly, to the uphill or downhill, softer sand or hard. We crest the hill that Paul had picked out—and we meet Maryanne, Jackie, and Christina coming from the opposite direction.

On top is a big hole twenty feet deep and twenty feet wide all around with a hint of remains of a wall, with sand piled all around the hole.

"It's a tomb," Paul explains. "They just aren't bothering with it because there are so many other big things. There's hundreds and hundreds of them out here."

How many hidden ancient treasures have Harry and I galloped over today?

Paul looks at me. "You want to go?" He read my mind! "This way!"

Off we canter over the desert to the distant Japanese Hill, near Abu Sir. It's the highest hill around, and you can see the pyramids of Giza, Abu Sir, Saqqara, and the Bent and Red and Melted Pyramids of Dashur, stretching north and south as far as we can see.

Harry poses proudly with me on top of the hill. He is extraordinarily photogenic, and so kind. Now I understand a little of the Egyptians' love affair and addiction to stallions, although I don't think there is another quite like Harry anywhere.

The magical ride is coming to an end. We trot on past the Abu Sir pyramids, heading back for the Sun Temple and the mango grove.

I eye the last hill between us and our exit from the desert. Harry must be thinking the same thing, because I just turn my hand, and my magnificent horse picks up an effortless lope to the top, and there we stop and look around the mystical Western Desert one last time together. I throw my arms around Harry's neck one last time, on top of the world in Egypt, staring down the mighty pyramids in all directions, and I murmur, "Shukran, Asal, Enta Gameel."

Thank You, my beautiful Honey in the desert.

Chapter 14—California

I wouldn't say I *enjoyed* it exactly, but I was getting more comfortable packing with our Forest Service horses in the backcountry. I still found it stressful, because I always thought of everything that could go wrong. I always retrospectively relished a pack trip when we stepped off the trail at the end and nothing had gone wrong.

I knew the Forest Service horses and Brenda the mule well, and we were buddies. Paiute was one of the best horses I'd ever ridden—still is. He could be a little spooky—at birds and squirrels hiding in bushes, and at the smell of bears, but I could always feel when a spook was coming, so I was always ready for it, and he never panicked. I liked Paiute so much that I forgave him when it took me forty-five minutes to catch him on days I needed him for leading the pack string, which is saying a lot, because that's one of my top pet peeves in naughty horse behavior. I trusted our horses and mule, and I was well aware of how lucky I was to have such good pack animals to work with and learn from.

But when our District Ranger suggested participating in the Bridgeport Fourth of July Parade, that threw me for a loop. "Wouldn't it be neat if we actually rode our Forest Service horses in it?"

Every year, small-town Bridgeport, the scenic gateway to the foothills of the Sierra Nevada Mountains in eastern California, put on a big-town holiday parade. For one day, the hikers hung up their backpacks, the fishermen put down their poles, and the boaters pulled into the docks, and they all headed into Bridgeport for a day of festivities. The BLM (Bureau of Land Management) and Forest Service employees costumed up and hopped on their floats (decorated flatbed trailers pulled by a truck), the Shriners fired up their old cars, the Hunewill Guest Ranch trailered in their horses and wranglers and weekly guests, and Leavitt Meadows Pack Station saddled up a string of packhorses and mules, for the parade down Main Street.

Our Forest Service horses certainly belonged in the parade: Forest and Park Services used to rely heavily on horse power on their trails, to pack rangers and gear and supplies into the backcountry. But horse use was becoming less and further between districts now. Bridgeport was one of the few districts in the Western U.S. that even had horses anymore.

It sounded good . . . but on second thought, though they were seasoned pack animals on mountain trails, we weren't sure how exactly our horses would take to sirens, horns, floats, flags, crowds of people, yelling children, and flying candy, much less on the paved streets of downtown Bridgeport.

We tossed around the idea of hauling them into town one quieter day for a practice run, but nobody ever had time, and we forgot about the whole thing.

And then July 3rd came about, and when I walked into the office that day, I heard the District Ranger and Range Con discussing the parade.

"I think we should go for it!" D.R. said. "What do you think?" she asked me.

Well, I was thinking of spooking horses on slick pavement, which was really hard if you fell off and hit it; of panicked horses tossing riders and getting loose . . .

"What the heck! Yeah, let's do it!" The novel idea of showing off our working Forest Service horses in a parade in front of lots of people was a thoroughly intriguing idea.

We drew up quick battle plans. I would not only ride the jumpiest horse, my buddy Paiute; I would also pony Zak, the half-blind one. Range Con would ride Redtop, and D.R.'s husband would ride Tom and pony Brenda the mule. D.R. would ride her own horse, one she sometimes endearingly referred to as a "Goofball." His real name was Boo. I thought neither name boded particularly well for a parade horse.

The only preparation we'd do would be to ride them down the back streets of town to get to the start of the parade—sort of a Crash Parade Test, although that was not the most auspicious description. If the horses couldn't make it one quiet block, we would skip the parade down Main Street and turn them right back around to their trailer.

July 4th

Our Forest Service horses were some pretty darn good pack and riding animals—smart, steady, strong, tolerant, and fairly bombproof. They'd faced deep streams, downed trees, booming thunderstorms, scary backpackers, a llama or two, and an occasional bear, all while maneuvering with heavy loads. They had no problems—in the forest and on mountain trails, that is. Except for that one time when Zak fell down the cliff a couple of years back, he'd never had any other problems, even when returning to that exact same spot, loaded with panniers.

On the morning of July 4th, we trailered the saddled horses to the east end of Bridgeport, and, with some human nerves a flutter, and a few horses' nerves a quiver, we mounted up and rode to the west end of town, on the paved back roads, to the beginning of the parade route. We would follow our Forest Service float, situated about in the middle of the string of floats in the parade.

The horses were all a little amped up with this new venue, feet clattering on the pavement, legs spinning—this sure didn't look like any pack trip they were familiar with. Paiute slipped on the slick pavement only once—but there was little traffic, and few people on the back road, and we arrived unscathed at our place in line in five minutes, where we joined our Forest Service float waiting in line. I'd even dressed up, in my long leather chaps, which I regularly wore packing, and a Forest Service pickle-green shirt, which I'd never worn in my life.

And there we waited. And waited. Paiute was tense and wide-eyed though he was able to stand still. I felt an occasional tremor jerk through his body, and he gave the occasional loud flared-nostril *SNOORRT* that some horses do when they are mighty suspicious of things.

Zak, standing beside us, was calm enough to close his eyes a few times. I knew he was going to wake up, once we got going. I wore gloves for the occasion, in case he tried ripping his lead rope out of my hand.

Boo was a nutcase; he couldn't stand still underneath D.R. for ten seconds. Range Con's Redtop was perfectly placid. Tom was shaking underneath D.R.'s husband, though he bravely stood still, and Brenda dozed off as Husband gave the insides of her big ears a good scratch. She was calm now, but Brenda was our Forest Service Wild Card.

Brenda had taught me a lot about mules. Mostly that you cannot outmuscle a mule like you can a horse, and you cannot make a mule do what a mule doesn't want to do. Hence: Wild Card. If you're lucky, you get to work with an affable, well-trained, highly intelligent mule like Brenda, who always agrees with what you're asking her to do, unless that's something like leading her to a veterinarian for a shot, in which case, she will turn around and drag you in the opposite direction from the needle. And who could fault her for that!

She'd always been such a gracious pack animal for me, but I had *no* idea what she would think of this parade. She might tag along behind Tom; she might be nervous and yank Husband right on out of the saddle and pull him back home; she might plant her feet and refuse to participate in the parade, and that would be that. I was secretly glad I was not leading Brenda!

The longer we waited, the bigger and rounder my buddy Paiute's eyes grew. From my seat on his back, it looked as if they might pop out the side of his head. He was very suspicious of what he might be standing there waiting for. He did look a pretty sight though, with his head high, ears pricked sharply forward, and his nostrils flaring.

After a good half hour of waiting, we finally started to move. "Uh oh, here we go!"

Husband took the lead with nervous high-stepping Tom, while Brenda serenely tagged along, game for anything—so far. Boo lived up to his name, goofily skittering sideways as if spooking from ghosts that none of the rest of us could see. Redtop plodded along, tranquil and steady, just as he did on the mountain trails. Paiute's wide eyes got even bigger as he danced his own two-step along the pavement; and while Zak was a little excited, the only thing he did was pull hard on his lead rope in my hand and try to keep his head even with Paiute. I tucked both boys in behind the calm Redtop and goofy Boo.

"Paiute," I instructed him, "now don't you be watching and copying Boo!"

As we turned the corner onto crowded Main Street, which normally doubled as eastern California's main north-south highway, I hunkered down in my saddle and hung on. Paiute's eyes were now definitely poking out of the side of his head. He didn't know which way to look or which side of the road lined with people to be more flustered about. *Ye gods!*—yelling kids here, waving and clapping fans there, fluttering things everywhere! He danced sideways this way and that, getting bouncier the more nervous he got. Zak wasn't scared—maybe it helped that his blind eye was outside facing the crowd, and he could keep his good eye on Paiute and me. Zak was just a little animated by all the commotion (including Paiute's), and when he stuck his head in front of Paiute, that really wigged Paiute out. I never felt Paiute would completely lose it, but I ignored the parade and concentrated very hard on my two horses—trying to keep Paiute going straight, and sometimes hauling back hard on Zak.

Paiute at first ping-ponged from one side of the road to the other, but each side was scarier than the next, and he deduced the middle half of the road was the safest bet, though he would not let his toes touch the sinister yellow horse-eating dividing lines painted down the center. I was able to keep him going fairly straight compared to Boo, who, to our right, was doing some mighty fine sidepassing to the left and right, left and right, as if he were a highly trained Lipizzaner dancing at the Spanish Riding School. D.R. was not asking him to do this, but she kept a grin on her face—or maybe she was gritting her teeth?—and kept waving to the crowd, while Range Con on ambling Redtop was able to wave gracefully at people like the Mayor of Bridgeport.

Up ahead of us, Husband was also concentrating on keeping nervous Tom calm, and then there was Brenda—Brenda! She was daintily sashaying along behind Tom, looking left and right, acknowledging her admiring fans by waving and waggling her huge ears.

This Fourth of July celebration was all about Brenda, our Queen of the Parade!

Halfway down Main Street the beginning of the parade turned around and doubled back toward us, approaching on our left. That's when it started getting hairy. Then we not only had the cheering fans on one side, but, coming *at* us on the other side— trucks! Floats! Noisy tractors shooting black smoke out their backsides! Little kids wearing fishes around their waists! (Very scary!) A string of eight pack mules! (Zak nickered at them). And then—oh help, miniature horses pulling miniature carts! All of our horses startled. Some of them slammed to a stop; others flew sideways. Paiute was one of the latter, shoving himself into Zak. Twelve bugged-out Forest Service packhorse eyes stared wildly at the tiny alien creatures. Never in their packhorse lives had they encountered shrunken horses with two extra legs made of wheels. All our Forest Service horses were freaked out—except for Brenda, who angled over toward them, because being the Queen of the Parade, she wanted to go make their acquaintance!

We successfully made it to the end of Main Street—halfway finished, and no accidents yet, a cause for celebration! Then we turned around to parade back. We still had cheering waving fans on our right, but now, not only were the scary little monster horses and carts ahead of us in sight, but also coming at us on the left were terrifying little pirates. They chanted Yo-Ho-Ho songs, threw candy, and drove noisy miniature cars; they whacked things along the street, tossed popping things—it was all too much for Tom. He started backing up in panic, and Husband spun him and Brenda (who wanted to join the games) and tucked him in behind us. That left crazy dancing Boo and D.R. in front of the strolling oblivious Redtop and waving Range Con, followed closely by a now-completely wigged out Paiute and an eagerly pulling Zak, followed by a freaking-out Tom and lightly dancing mule who was thoroughly enjoying her personal parade, which was *obviously* a tribute to the revered Mule breed.

During the whole ordeal I kept talking to Paiute and Zak, telling them how brave they were, reaching down to pet them both during the few moments when I could ease up on the reins and lead rope. Zak believed me, but Paiute was pretty convinced he'd gone to horse hell for the day.

There must have been a couple hundred people watching this little hometown parade. I heard my name a few times but only looked up twice, because I didn't dare take my eyes off my two horses. Someone yelled at me to smile, and I thought I did, or possibly I showed my clenched teeth in response. There were too many little kids running around to get the flying candy—way too close to the horses—and I was focused on keeping Paiute just under panic mode and going in as straight a line as possible, and keeping Zak a head behind him. This Parade was fun . . . *sure* it was!

We'd almost reached the end of the parade and the turn off of Main Street, when here came the California Highway Patrol and Deputy Sheriffs, and an ambulance, a late addition to the festivities, with not only their lights flashing, but their sirens wailing on full blast. Oh, how convenient! When I got thrown onto the cement and trampled, they could just keep those lights and sirens on, and toss me in the back, and drive on to the hospital in the next town, without slowing down!

But after the trauma of little kids wearing fishes, popping pirates, and peewee horses with wheels, screaming cars were nothing. Our brave horses did not even blink at those. We successfully reached the end of Bridgeport and the end of our first Fourth of July parade, and once we turned off Main Street, and left the parade monsters behind, our horses calmed down considerably.

We had done it. They had survived it—the first Parade of the Bridgeport Forest Service horses! And a new Parade Queen was crowned today—Brenda the Mule!

Chapter 15—Egypt

MY KING

"Come over and ride with us!" said Paul, over the phone.

I walked the half mile along the canal road and down a dusty lane to Paul's stables, imagining our fun ride galloping in the desert by pyramids. These were two of the main reasons I'd returned to Egypt: the horses and the pyramids.

Paul's Egyptian grooms were busy tacking horses for the four of us. "You'll ride Borcan," Paul said.

I stopped short as my daydreams rapidly evaporated. *Borcan!*

My nerves fluttered at the thought: Borcan, the blustery, formidable, woman-hating, breast-biting ("He's bitten three breasts so far," Paul declared adoringly) white stallion in the paddock next to the sweet chestnut stallion Shams, whom Paul would be riding. Jeannie would be aboard a young filly, and Paul would give a riding lesson to Katherina, aboard Prince.

The Breast-Biter himself was already tacked up and standing at his paddock fence, with his lips peeled back to expose his enormous nine-year-old teeth, which were grabbing one of his reins and clamping down tightly, grinding the rubber till it squeaked in protest, exhibiting what he'd do to me if he managed to get a hold of my breast. Clearly a demonstration of equine foreplay.

Let's see: a ride in the desert with a young filly, a green rider, and two stallions . . . one of whom was this fearsome biter that *I* would be riding. Was this a good idea? These thoughts waved big red flags in my head, but I was too timid to voice my concerns aloud, because I desperately wanted to ride in the desert again!

I'd seen the way Borcan lunged, teeth bared, if one got too close to him; and I'd even seen him go after Paul, his owner; so I always gave him a good berth at his fence. I never bothered trying to pet him like one could most typical sensible horses. Shams, in the next paddock, was so kind and gentle, one would never know he was a stallion, nor that he was so abused by an evil man only five years earlier that he had every right to hate humankind.

I had also noticed, however, that while Borcan put on a show of trying to savage Paul, he was very vigilant not to *actually* bite him. He would dive big teeth-first open-mouthed at Paul, and when Paul raised his hands, fearlessly *inviting* him closer, Borcan's teeth would be closed when they hit Paul's hands. Borcan pinned his ears fiercely, and peeled his lips back in a threat, but he never opened his teeth to bite his owner.

"You take their anger, and turn it to play," Paul explained simply.

"Riiiight . . ." I'd answered.

Borcan sure scared *me*. He also had his reasons for disliking people—particularly women. He'd been abused when he was younger, by a woman who had trained him to "dance," a movement similar to the piaffe in dressage, trotting in place in time to music. The dancing horses in Egypt are trained for special occasions or competitions using various methods of persuasion.

"They used hooks on him. You can still see some of the scars," Paul said, pointing them out. No wonder Borcan hated females, and knew how to get them back where it hurt.

It was obvious Borcan loved Paul, and Paul definitely doted on this blusterball—and in fact all of his horses. Norwegian Paul was one of the happiest middle-aged little boys I had ever had the pleasure to know. His wife was the Norwegian ambassador to Ethiopia, and while she was away, Paul played with his beloved horses. Just ask one little question about his kids—his horses—and his eyes widened and sparkled like sapphires and his face beamed with proud delight. Pull up a chair on his porch, above his stables, and he'll serve you a great cup of Ethiopian coffee (or a good cold beer), and instead of pulling out his wallet and dropping an accordion sheet of photos, he will point to his horses in the paddocks below and tick off their accomplishments as proudly as a father giving you a blow by blow of his kids' soccer games.

I couldn't get quite as smitten by Borcan's antics. I'd witnessed how excited the stallion got when Paul climbed aboard his back; I'd seen how he swelled to a monster twice his normal size, physically and mentally, half rearing, prancing like a naughty juvenile show horse out the long driveway, whipping his butt back and forth, while the other imperturbable horses like Prince and Shams poked along at a relaxed, civilized walk far behind him.

Was it too late to back out of riding? Surely, I reasoned, Paul would not put me on a horse that would hurt me. And I *really* wanted to ride in the desert.

Still too cowardly to admit I was a little scared, I instead had a little discussion with Borcan out of earshot of Paul. I told him that even though I might look it, I really was not a hateable female, and, "Please," I whispered to him, "please don't toss me on the pavement, or in a canal, or out in the desert so you can trample me or shred me with your teeth!"

Borcan ignored me and continued biting the daylights out of his rein, not even letting go when I reached over and took hold of the rein and tried to pull, then yank, it out of his mighty mouth. He even disdainfully ignored me when I dared to pet his neck while he was so passionately occupied with the Death Bite on the rubber. He did not reach over to savage my arm, or some other offending female body part; but he continued to exhibit to me that if he *did* decide to get a hold of me, I would be a delicious hors d'oeuvre. I was sufficiently wary and possibly frightened, and that ended our talk.

The groom himself had to be leery of Borcan's teeth sinking into his arm, as he held the ferocious stallion for me to mount. I said a quick little prayer as the groom legged me up. After landing on his back, I found the stirrups too short; so Borcan graciously stood still and occupied himself with trying to bite his martingale instead of the groom, or my legs, as I moved them forward for the groom to work on the stirrups.

Once that was fixed, no one else had mounted yet, but, how silly it was of me to think that Borcan would have any interest in continuing to stand still and wait—that was far beneath his Great White Dignity. Oh, no, it was time for the Great White Peacock

Parade down the long drive. Neck bowed, white mane billowing, Borcan consented to a walk, but only so everybody could get a very long look at his magnificence. He strutted, he waltzed, he erupted with absolute equine masculinity.

And there you have it—against my better judgment, I had already fallen for him. He was such a blustery show off, but he was simply magnificently breathtaking, especially from his back (where he couldn't bite me). I couldn't help but reach down and rough up his gorgeous long mane, which he only took as his due—pure adulation from the girly peon on his back—and he bowed his neck tighter and shook his head, lashing that silky mane about. He knew exactly what he was doing and how he looked. Television starlets flicking their long hair had nothing on this ostentatious equine.

We got to the end of the drive, and still nobody else had even started after us yet, so I turned Borcan around so he could show off some more. Borcan swaggered back to the stables, where his minions were now mounted and beginning to follow; and this time there was no mistaking or ignoring who was the Great White King of the Egyptian-Norwegian castle.

Borcan led the grand procession down the drive, bouncing on his toes, whipping his tail, dancing and prancing and shaking his head. He was feeling so darn good about his almighty self, and I was so secretly loving being his totally insignificant passenger who looked like an experienced rider on such a tempestuous stallion, that I let him waltz along till we far outdistanced the others.

My white stallion flitted by the fellahin in the fields and gallivanted past the gamoosas in the gardens, hoping they would notice his ferociousness. But the fellahin were busy harvesting crops for the practicalities of life, and the gamoosas were busy eating and flicking flies away with their tails, and none took notice of a haughty blowhard white stallion clattering noisily down the dusty roads, though perhaps they did glance up once in a while to see whether the sufficiently cowed foreign girl rider on his back might be tossed off into the slimy canal, near the edges of which Borcan's hooves danced dangerously closely.

Borcan and I turned back yet again to meet the others, who were still walking pragmatically and calmly far behind us, then we turned once more and cavorted in front, leading the way across the main canal road, alongside another larger, daunting canal. We passed waving Egyptian children with brilliant smiles, and women wearing brightly colored galabiyas, carrying water jugs balanced on their heads. The children yelled, "Hello! Hello!" and I dared let go of a rein with one hand to wave and smile and say, "As-salaam alaikum!"

My hand would then automatically fall to Borcan's beautifully curved neck, and he would puff up just a little bigger, and skitter just a little faster and tougher down the lane so that I had to grab the reins with two hands again to hold him in check, which made him look even more superbly powerful and beautiful.

We jigged toward the desert far in front of the other less beautiful dawdling plugs. Shoving open a gate, we burst into the lane that led through and past Ali's stables, where the Western Desert loomed in front of us. Borcan forgot his horse brethren, broke into a trot with Great White Purpose toward the desert, ready to open his Great White Wings, to soar with splendid majesty over the Great Sands of Egypt . . .

. . . and I almost flew up onto his neck as he hauled on the brakes so he could mark his territory on a poop pile. Since the other horses had yet to catch up with us, I let Borcan have his way, sniffing the interloper's pile of poop in his Great Desert. He moved forward, then backward, positioning himself just so, and crapped all over it. *Take that!* Then he turned around, put his head down, sniffed everything long and hard to make sure he had made the most flawless statement; and Borcan found himself quite satisfied with life.

Shams and Paul were just catching up with us, so Borcan lifted his head, puffed himself back up, and leaned in menacingly toward Shams (who ignored him). Then he bore in toward the paddock fence which contained a gray (totally uninterested) gelding, and he fluffed himself up even bigger as he rolled his eyes between the oblivious gelding and heedless Shams, and he leered at the gray filly (who didn't notice).

My legendary (in his mind) stallion leaped in front again, leading the way into the desert, then, whoa! Another poop pile to sniff and crap on once more, to reinforce the boundaries of his territory and the masterful assertion of his superiority! Everybody passed us as Borcan worked diligently on this exceedingly important task. Once accomplished, we trotted to catch up with the others, Borcan all fluffed up and looking grand for having crapped twice now (nobody noticed).

I figured that now, my mighty powerful Great White King and I would get on with the business of conquering the desert, but Borcan had cast his attention about to other crap piles—there were hundreds, thousands, millions of them, scattered over the Sahara sand like stars in the Egyptian night sky.

When he stopped to crap on the next nearest pile, "*Enough*, Borcan!" I told him, nudging him with my heels. He moved onward, miffed, because this was *really important*, and how would I, the insignificant girl on his back, ever understand such significant stallion protocol?

Now, with his focus somewhat forcibly directed forward and upward, we could go attack the desert. I had hoped the mighty Borcan would not be too uncontrollable. But when the Great White King reached the open desert, I was in the opposite predicament. With thousands of miles of nothing but sand in front of him—heavy sand that it would take a bit of effort to get over—Borcan's Great White Purpose for Being (showing off) shriveled, and between my legs he abruptly morphed into a total pansy.

Borcan noticed when the gallop became a little too fast or the slope was a little too much uphill or the sand was too deep. It dawned on him that it was dreadfully hot and humid. And the flies, oh, the wretched flies, oh Misery! It was not possible to canter on Borcan, because while moving, he kicked at his belly and snapped at his chest and swished his tail in colossal agitation at flies, real or imagined. I suspected most of them were not real—*I* didn't see any flies. I felt he might trip and fall over.

It was a good thing that we weren't going on a fast ride today, since Katherina was a beginning rider, which suited Borcan just fine. Paul's instructions to me were to keep Borcan a bit apart from everybody, which suited *me* just fine. Jeannie was riding a four-year-old filly, which may very well have put Borcan in the mood to fight with Prince (who, gelded, could have cared less), and Shams (who, though a stallion, simply had more manners).

So Borcan was free, on this easy ride, to be in front, and not have to work too hard at staying up there. He threw his big white butt side to side like a model on the runway, which made him look *really* hot in front of Jeannie's filly (who could have cared less).

There were a few rare moments when we were strutting ahead, when Borcan would forget about showing off. Then he'd relax to a normal walk or trot, watch a rolling plastic bag in the breeze, have a look at the picturesque desert around him, glance at the line of pyramids that were unusually sharp today in the clear desert air.

Then he'd catch a glimpse of the gray filly behind him and remember his Great White Purpose in Life—looking good—and he'd puff himself back up, bow his neck, and whip his lustrous tail and flip his luscious mane along his muscular neck.

We worked our way up into the sand hill quarries where Paul picked a little hill and ditch to train on—training for the inexperienced Katherina on Prince, who was testing his rider, and for the inexperienced gray filly, who'd only been out in the desert three times before.

Borcan and I were supposed to wait while Paul gave instructions, but standing still in one spot was not one of Borcan's specialties. He wanted to move, to dance, to pivot closer to Shams so he could fight or show off. I wanted him to stand still.

After discussing it a bit, we reached a sort of compromise. Borcan kept his feet in one place while he fidgeted with his upper body: he bit his own chest. He bowed his neck like a pretzel, reached down, using those big white teeth, took a mouthful of his chest, and clamped down hard with the Death Bite. He first bit one side of his chest, then he flung his head straight up high in the air and back down to the other side, and bit the other side of his chest, hard. I could hear his skin squeaking in protest, like I heard his reins squeaking before our ride! Back and forth, he threw his head up in the air and then down, administering the Death Bite *to his own chest*.

I was somewhat aghast. "Uh . . . Paul . . ." I called.

Paul looked over at us, said adoringly, "Oh, he's just sucking his thumb!"

Borcan was quite aware of how resplendent he looked when he tossed his long locks about, but neither he (nor Paul) seemed to realize that his thumb-sucking chest-biting stunt detracted greatly from his masculinity. It also astounded me that he could bite himself so dang hard without a whimper, but earlier in the ride, a teensy-weensy possibly imagined fly bite caused him such wretchedness.

"You Big Queen!" I said, roughing up Borcan's mane, stroking his neck, but nothing distracted him from the Death Bites. He really was a beautiful stallion—gleaming white in the direct sunshine, with little faint brown spots all over, which subtly matched the tan and russet Egyptian sands. I kept running my fingers through his silken mane (he didn't mind at all, since I obviously worshiped him), which was flecked with blond and gold hairs.

Obstacle lessons over, Borcan stopped biting his chest and leapt to the front of our group as we made a loop through the sand quarries, and back toward home. We crested Japanese Hill, where we had a broad view of the Abu Sir Pyramids on the right, the open desert to the left, and straight ahead in the distance, the pyramids of Giza. Here we usually broke into a gallop over the inviting flat sand.

However, I was riding Queen Borcan, who really had no interest in putting forth the effort to try and keep up with the other horses, since looking good was highest on his priority list, and running behind horses did not in any way support that effort.

We were being left behind with each stride. I smooched to him, and nudged his wussy sides with my heels, and he unbecomingly grunted, but didn't pick up the pace from a slow canter. The only reason we eventually caught up with our stable mates was because they had slowed to a walk.

A half mile from our desert exit, however, we came over a little rise and spotted a couple of horses—tourists out for a ride—and Borcan blossomed back into a gorgeous white masculine athletic stallion, all inflated and available for the fillies in the string. He pranced and jigged and bowed his neck and cantered in place (you think I could get him to stop cantering now?), rolling his eyes over there to make sure they were all watching spellbound (unlikely). As they passed us, I let Borcan stop and turn around so he could watch them turn around and watch him (they didn't.)

Just fifty yards from Ali's stables, Borcan bolted ahead of everybody and then stopped at his own last crap pile, and left another pertinent message. He was once again: Borcan, the Great White King of the Desert!

And he led the parade back home—clattering down the roads, sashaying that Great White Butt, swaggering past the fellahin, sneering at the gamoosas, and exploding in a Great White Cloud of Glory as he arrived at his castle, in the lead, full of glorious tales of his Great White Desert Prowess to tell his stable mates, who would all be sufficiently impressed.

Chapter 16—Egypt

MY ROCKET SHIP

Eighteen-year-old Prince pinned his ears as I crouched over his neck, moving with his rhythm, urging him on. He pounded the sand at a hard run, trying to keep up with Raad. Raad, the steel-gray half-Arabian four-year-old colt ahead of us with Paul leaning forward into his mane, had his ears pricked forward, and was gliding over the sand faster, pulling away from us with every stride, no effort involved. Jeannie and Katir followed far behind us at a more sane canter.

We all slowed to a walk to give the horses a breather as we passed the Saqqara complex and its mystical Step Pyramid of Djoser. I could not turn my eyes away from it—I was riding a Prince by the forty-six hundred-year-old tomb of a God-King.

Jeannie turned her horse westward to canter up the big wadi toward Magdy's hill. Paul and I let her go, watching her, talking horses, until she became a speck in the desert. It was a game of tag you got to play when you rode with Paul, who loved to play with his horses in the desert: let somebody go, go catch them. Keep going, let them catch up with you.

Paul turned Raad loose and let him run, heading toward the distant speck. I let Prince do as he wished, which was a hand gallop. He was no longer interested in trying to catch that gray lightning bolt, probably because it was a lost cause. Prince was quick on his feet, but he wasn't *that* fast. Where once I'd been afraid to gallop, I felt quite safe on Prince. What Prince was doing with me seemed so . . . *tame* compared to Raad. Watching Raad shoot away put a *whole* new perspective on galloping a horse.

Eventually Prince and I caught up with Jeannie and Katir, who had slowed to a walk, and together we watched Raad and Paul continue running, bearing off to the right, still at a dead run, making a huge arc out in the wide open desert, eventually coming back around full circle to join up with us again. That was the great thing about this part of the Western Desert—you could go running off anywhere you wanted whenever the whim struck you.

Raad slowed down as he approached us. I thought Paul's trajectory had been for fun, but in fact, he hadn't been arcing on a whim.

"This! (pant!) . . ."

"Horse! (pant!) . . ."

"Is! (pant!) . . ."

"SO STRONG!" Paul gasped. "I couldn't steer him!"

I thought he was kidding. Paul was a good rider, and he rode his horses on a light rein, whomever he was riding or however fast he was going. He'd given me some pointers on how to ride "light"—but it usually didn't work for me. I still had a lot to learn about riding, although I was delighting in the fact that, finally, I loved, *loved* to gallop out here in the desert because I wasn't afraid to do it anymore.

Paul shook his head in utter bliss, his eyes gleaming. "That's the Akhal-teke in him. They are so strong—and strong minded—they don't bloody listen!" he said with unmistakable pride in his voice. But then, Paul so loved all his horses, anything they did just tickled him.

I was glad I wasn't riding Raad; if Paul couldn't control him, I'd have had no chance in holding him back.

Paul turned to me. "You want to try him?"

My eyes widened. Too strong for Paul? Can't steer him? Can't pull him up?

"Yeah!"

We hopped off our horses, adjusted the stirrups, and I climbed on the big gray powerful tank of horseflesh.

We gathered our reins, Paul said, "Hah, Prince!" and Prince leaped to a canter. And I was—

GONE.

Raad leapt to a canter, and shifted to a gallop, then to a flat out run in two strides.

OH!

MY!

GOD!

I was hanging onto a rocket ship streaking over the desert. Raad was so light on his feet and powerful—and *FAST*. Never had I experienced anything like this staggering speed. And, my God, he was so smooth! We hurtled over the sand, impossibly, blisteringly fast, wind screaming in my ears, gray mane slashing me silly in the face as I leaned forward over my bullet roaring over the desert, the others already far behind us in a swirl of still-settling sand.

I had absolutely no control over this unearthly creature and I did not care. He was so fast he blasted any "scared" I might have had away. There was no slowing or steering him, even if I had wanted; I could only hold on and not interfere with him. I was stunned by his force. I was thrilled by his power. And like Paul, I could only coax him into a very large arc back toward the others. We raced toward Morocco, soared toward the Mediterranean, swooped back to Egypt and the pyramids, and approached our mortal companions.

Raad slowed himself down when we got near the others.

"Would!" yelled Paul . . .

"You! . . ."

"Wipe that silly grin off your face!" he laughed, echoing my own apparently insane grin. I couldn't get any words out of my gaping mouth. I shook my head in absolute awe.

We jigged alongside Prince and Katir for a while, but . . .

. . . there was this long, empty, inviting road-like impression in the sand along this wide open, inviting desert wadi, in this wide open Egyptian desert of pyramids, and Raad and I couldn't help ourselves. We blasted off again. This horse was pure muscle, speed, power—he ran for the sheer fun of it, because he *could*.

We ran, and ran, before Raad agreed to slow down as we headed uphill. On top, we came to a stop, and we turned to wait and eventually watch the other two trot up to join us. Raad's breath billowed in and out as he stared imperiously over the others. Our three horses wandered around on top of the hill, Prince leading the way, and Raad revving up, trying to leap into a canter after him, me trying to wrestle him down to a trot.

At the bottom of the hill, we were pointed west again, toward open desert . . . Prince started trotting, Raad sprang to a canter, and, well . . . the temptation was too great . . . but I could not have resisted if I had tried.

"All right, go on then!" I yelled—as if I had any say in the matter—and we were gone instantly, a great gray missile rocketing over the surface of the sand. I was so completely insignificant to his being. Such unbelievable force, absolutely no control—I was in serious danger of overdosing on this magnificent beast. Raad disdained the earth, skimming above it, leaving fire in his wake. He could soar into the heavens and shoot among the stars if he so desired. Running, *running*, in an intoxicating rush. I could not get enough of him. Breathtaking, delirious, seductive power, faster than I'd ever gone in my life, flying on a horse, *with no fear.*

I came back to my senses. This was not my horse. I did not want to hurt him. I tried to slow Raad, and he eased up to a fast gallop—then decided he'd run again. Once more, I had to let him go, and go . . . or did I? . . . and finally pulled myself back from the brink again.

I *had* to slow him down. I pulled and pulled on his reins, and wore myself out, as he slowly roared to a canter, then a trot and a walk, his engines revving down, our joined heart rates slowing, the rush slowly ebbing.

MY GOD!

We trotted our way back to Paul and Jeannie, a nice long earth-eating trot, still gliding over the sand, Raad bowing his thick powerful neck, listening to me, just because he decided he would, not because of any magical communication I had developed with this exciting creature.

"He's much lighter with you than he is with me," Paul said.

What? Paul must not have noticed I totally had no control over his beloved Raad, whom he'd raised as a baby and trained, and who could do no wrong.

Paul led the way through the sand quarries on Prince, followed by Jeannie and Katir, while behind them, I desperately scuffled with Raad, who wanted to blow by the other two again.

This was the same situation I'd been in on Fred so long ago, when I'd had my first gallop on a racehorse. No control, and desperate for my horse not to bolt into a run. Only this time, even though this horse was so much more powerful and unearthly than Fred, God knows why, I wasn't scared.

I wasn't scared! If I had any sense, I *would* have been afraid on such a strong beast, but the fact was that it was embarrassment, and not fear, making me desperate and giving me extra strength. I didn't want my horse to bolt by Paul and race home with me hanging on like a feather, now that Paul had said we were "light" and all.

By now, my whole body was pooped from grappling against Raad's raw strength—my legs were shot, my arms whooped; the reins were rubbing my fingers raw, and I was panting as if *I* had run to Morocco in the sand.

Behind Prince and Katir, I seesawed on Raad's mouth and put my whole body weight behind it—I meant business this time! *No blowing by your owner!* I told him with my hands, my weight, my legs, and my silent voice. If Raad jumped to a gallop again I was a goner— I simply would not have the strength left to pull him up this time, and it sure felt as if he could run for days without stopping.

Nearing home, Prince and Katir picked up a trot, and Raad took that as an excuse to jump into a canter. I superhumanly cranked his head to the left, keeping an anchor rein on him, trying to tuck him behind Katir and Prince. That horse could canter well with his head turned over ninety degrees from his body. By now, my legs were trembling, my arms shaking at the end of the reins, and a couple of my fingers were bleeding. (Mental note: wear gloves next time when riding a rocket ship!)

Oh, it would have been so easy, so . . . fatal . . . to let Raad go—just one more time—and stop the fighting—just one more rush—but I didn't dare.

The iron God-Horse and I fought with each other, physically and mentally—but I managed to keep him from bolting, and as we got to Ali's place where we left the desert, Raad finally relaxed and came back to earth as a regular horse.

When I slithered off him at Paul's house, my legs nearly collapsed beneath me.

Not from fear or defeat.

From exciting, absolute triumph: a truly fulfilled dream from long ago.

The Boogey Man was gone!

Chapter 17—California

THE LAST RIDE

It is my fourth year in a row to ride the trails of the Eastern High Sierra Classic in California's Sierra Nevada Mountains. One of the most scenic endurance rides in the country, it's a challenging 50-mile trail; but a carefully ridden, fit horse can handle it in stride.

Last year I rode my pal Zayante. This year I am riding my pal Raffiq, owned by Gretchen. She's riding her other horse Spice; we are riding with Hiromi, from Japan, on Jackie's horse Zayante. The horses are great buddies, particularly Raffiq and Zayante. Raffiq so loves Zayante, he will scream all night long for his buddy if they are out of eyesight of each other in Ridecamp. We tried that at one ride and we will not do that again for fear of being run out of town!

Raffiq has finished this ride five times in a row. He's working on 2600 career endurance miles. Spice is the "Newbie" to endurance. It's only her second Eastern High Sierra Classic, and her 300th mile in her third year of endurance. Zayante is working on his 13,250th mile today. He's never looked better over the years. Zayante has finished this particular ride seven times—not to mention all the years and miles that he's marked, and unmarked trails just for the ride.

A golden sunrise escorts us up into the mountains on the first loop. We start mid-pack, going our usual easy pace—there is a lot of elevation gain and technical terrain to traverse—as none of us are after anything other than a good, safe, enjoyable ride and a finish.

Our trail becomes ever more scenic, the higher we climb: views of the jagged snow-kissed Matterhorn Peak ahead of us, and the deep blue alpine Twin Lakes far below us; and spread out beyond, the Hoover Wilderness, trails I know well from packing with the Forest Service horses.

Our horses handle the ground and altitude and home trails easily. At the first vet check back in base camp, they all look sound and free flowing in their trot outs, and they drink well and consume a hearty meal of grain, and all the hay they want to eat.

It's a long haul up the first half of that second loop toward Eagle Peak. Walking the steep climbs and trotting the flats, we walk downhill, and dismount to lead our horses when the trails become steep or rocky. We wind up, then down, through the Jeffrey pine, white fir, and aspen groves.

Passing through where our next vet check will be after an out-and-back loop, we pause to let the horses snack, and to have our friend Heather take pictures of us on this amazing ride. The next part of the loop will take us six flat and easy miles up Buckeye Canyon, and six miles back, into this last vet check and hold before the finish.

Our horses trot along easily, slowing to a walk every once in a while if the trail becomes rocky, then picking up an effortless trot again. We'd dropped back to mid-back of the pack, but, who was in a big hurry? It is such a gorgeous day, and we are having fun, although I am keeping an eye on those suspicious blue puffy clouds slowly beginning to form over the north side of the canyon. Bridgeport tends to get thunderstorms this time of year late in the afternoon, and I tend to be quite afraid of lightning.

We have just about an hour out, and an hour back to the vet check, I figure—we'll make it in time to miss any thunderstorms. The horses look and feel great—Raffiq is happy to be following his much-adored Zayante's white butt, and I myself admire Zayante's willing, floating trot in front of us. Seven hundred endurance miles I'd ridden Zayante—the best endurance horse I'd ever been on—and how many countless miles I have followed alongside or behind him, admiring this same enthusiastic energizer-bunny trot he is showing today, his forward-pricked ears, and his grand horse-terrorizing sneer he often turns upon fellow equines who have the gall to pass us.

We stop at the little creeks flowing across our path and let the horses drink or nose about for grass bites. At the Buckeye river crossing on the furthest point of the loop, we pause to let two other riders cross before us. Spice and Raffiq shove their noses down into the grass for a snack. Zayante will have none of that; he wants to continue. This is no time to eat; this is an endurance ride! He keeps walking impatiently in circles.

Then he paws the ground, an odd thing for him to do.

Then he crouches. "No!" Hiromi says, and immediately jumps off him.

Zayante crouches again—and it slams us: Zayante is *trying to go down.*

Oh, dear God, no.

Colic we all think—but at the same time, we are all in denial, as this cannot be possible, Zayante colicking, on top of Zayante colicking at the worst possible place, six miles from the nearest veterinarian.

In fifteen seasons of campaigning, over 13,000 miles, over two hundred starts, Zayante has never once had a metabolic problem, so, truly, this cannot be possible; and yet, here we are, faced with a terrifying catastrophe. But it can't be, can it? While our minds are in denial, our gut reactions kick in.

I hear words come out of my mouth that sound like the right thing to do.

"Get back on, Hiromi, if he's colicking, we have got to get him walking back to the vet!" The vet, who is six miles away, and at a walk, nearly two hours away. We ride across the river and start back down the trail. Zayante does not want to walk; he wants to hurry up and run. Hiromi keeps him tucked behind Spice's butt, but he does his Zayante jig, which cannot be converted to a walk. When he does have to slow down to step over rocks, he tries to squat down, and Hiromi yanks upward on his reins, and yelps at him to stay up and on his feet and keep moving.

Following behind them on Raffiq, my mind can still not comprehend that my pal Zayante is colicking—surely it will just go away! It had come on so suddenly; it could go away just as quickly, couldn't it? The day had been great, we were having a great time, and nothing in the world was wrong; so this just cannot be happening.

As we move along, Zayante becomes more insistent about trying to go down. Hiromi says, "I'll get off and try to lead him."

The instant she jumps off, he falls to his knees. She yells at Zayante and yanks him up; not really thinking, I lean from Raffiq and grab Zay's lead rope: "Let me try ponying him!"

Raffiq hasn't ever taken to ponying horses, and here, amidst such tumult of yelling and stressed humans and one human on foot and one terribly stressed alien horse, he doesn't take to it either. Raffiq's instinct in certain unpleasant situations is to bolt. He tries to do so here, his front end climbing, his head up in the air. I have an anchor hold on his reins with my left hand but cannot pay attention to him anyway because I am holding onto a calamity in my right hand.

I am in a quandary: in my limited experience with colic, I know Zayante probably should be walking. But walking him is impossible; he refuses to walk, and if we slow too much he tries to go down; and my instinct says he doesn't have the time left to walk in. At a walk, we are still at least over an hour and a half from the vet. *My God*, I think, *what do I do? If this is colic, and his gut is twisted, will trotting him make it worse? Will I kill Zayante by trotting him? Will I kill him if I make him walk? Does he have that much time left?*

The full impact hits me like a physical blow: We are impossibly too far away from help, and my buddy Zayante may die out here.

I turn back to Gretchen in despair: "I don't know what to do. *I just don't know what to do!*"

"Just keep going," Gretchen says; and we keep going, because there is nothing else we can do, trying to keep up a slow trot.

I ride through a nightmare of despair. I am aware that Zayante is in great pain. His ears are pinned flat, his mouth curled in a great grimace: not his competitive sneer, but one of suffering. He throws his head down, yanking me downward in the saddle. He turns to Raffiq and tries to savage him in the neck, in the face. He thrusts his head in front of Raffiq's head, trying to run off. He begins to huff and puff with every diagonal hoof beat—like he does when he is digging in and expending great effort powering up a steep hill.

I fight off the thought that tries to take over my mind, that this is not going to work, we are not going to make it. Raffiq is freaking out, trying to run off. Beside him is his best buddy in the whole world, Zayante, his friend who he will whinny for an entire twelve-hour night in Ridecamp. But this is not the Zayante he knows:

this Zay is leaning on him, hanging onto him, biting him, trying to out-run him.

I am leaning hard on Raffiq to counter Zayante's weight and to hold Zay back because he just wants to run, or to plunge to the earth away from this terrible pain. I am the only thing holding Zayante up on his four feet. My muscles are getting tired, I am panting from the exertion; but if we slow down, Zay tries to buckle under.

We still have at least thirty minutes to go, and I start to despair because I can't possibly keep up this muscling for that long because I will collapse—my arms will just quit working and I'll lose my reins and Raffiq will run off and I will lose hold of Zay's lead rope and he will go down, and when he goes down we will not get him up again, and he will die out here on this trail, miles from the vet.

Zayante tries to go down at the trot. Hiromi yells at him and smacks him in the belly and the butt; I yell at him and roughly yank on his halter to get his head up, curse him, curse my beloved Zayante, *"Don't you go down on me, don't you FUCKING die on me,"* angrily, because it keeps back the tears which will make me give up and all will be lost. I see Hiromi—she has been running on foot beside us the whole way, for miles now. If Hiromi can keep running right beside Zay, I can keep holding on a little longer.

We are still forever away from the vet check. My muscles are screaming now. Zayante is hanging heavily on us, yanking his head down hard as if he wants to crash straight into the ground at the trot. I hold his head up, crying at the effort, but my right hand is cramping; I am losing the grip on his lead rope, my fingers will no longer close around it—one more hard pull and I will lose Zayante. I jam a finger into the knot on the bottom of his halter and grasp him that way. My left arm holding Raffiq back is about to give out. I pray for strength to whoever is listening, and from my mouth, I croak the words that have been spinning through my mind: "Gretchen—*I can't do this any longer."*

"Yes, you can, we're close," she encourages, her voice calm and steady. "What can I do? Do you want me to try and pony him?"

What can you do? Send me a savior—Nick and Judy are riding behind us, they will catch up and Nick will know what to do, he will make everything better, he will help. Nick loves Zayante as much as I do. *Oh God*, I think, *no, don't let Nick see this, it will kill him.* Nick and Judy are an hour behind us anyway, too far back to help.

What can you do? I would love for Gretchen to pony Zayante, but Spice doesn't pony horses, and we cannot stop to switch horses anyway, because Zayante will go down if we stop.

There will be no help; it is Gretchen and Hiromi and me and Raffiq and Spice left to save Zayante with whatever decisions we make.

"Set the pace," I gasp. "Put Spice in front of Raffiq."

And Gretchen moves Spice in front of us—Spice who still does not have a steady trot because she either goes too fast or too slow, and she doesn't like another horse right on her butt—but Gretchen sets her on the perfect pace, a slow trot, right in front of Raffiq, who calms down a bit with his buddy Spice right in front of him. It gives some relief to my shrieking fatigued left arm anyway.

In these terrible last few miles, I have been completely ignoring Raffiq; I have been riding him by instinct, and riding him roughly. Normally I am hands-on with the horses I ride—I praise them with my voice and hands. Raffiq is used to me telling him he's a good boy vocally, and by petting him, and using a soft hand on his reins. I often drop the reins and stroke his neck with both of my hands as we are trotting along. But here I am yelling and cursing at Zay, yanking on Raffiq's reins when he tries to bolt or shy away from Zay, kicking Raffiq hard in the left side to counter Zay's leaning force or biting teeth on the right; I can only change my voice from a snarling curse at Zay to a strangled panting "Good boy, Raffiq" and back to a "GET UP!" growl at Zay.

I no longer know how many miles we have gone, how many we have left; I don't see how we will make it. I viscerally feel Zayante's awful pain; but I can do nothing for it, and I have a terrible feeling that I am the one killing him, because I have only two choices—go fast or go slow—and I might be choosing to do the wrong thing.

A group of riders pass us a couple of miles from the vet check, and we tell them Zayante is colicking, we need a vet, tell a vet to be ready. They ride on ahead, and our group struggles onward.

We are still too far away. I am out of breath, out of strength, grunting every time Zayante lunges ground-ward, cursing Zayante, telling him, "You can do it, Buddy"—but when I think I won't last any longer, I look over and see Hiromi, *still* running beside Zayante, still yelling at him and swatting him when he wants to go down, encouraging him, rubbing his belly and his back as we trot along. She sprints ahead to open gates we must continue trotting through, and after she closes the gates she sprints back to Zayante's side, pushing him on, humming to him, yelling at him, petting him, whacking him while jogging beside him. And Gretchen is still the steady rock in front of me and Raffiq, keeping Raffiq from bolting, telling me that I can do it, that we are almost there, as I curse Zayante again and roughly yank his head back up from the ground.

Then Jane and a friend come riding up behind us about a half mile out from the vet check. "Tell them Zayante is colicking, we need a vet—tell a vet to meet us at the gate!" we plead. Finally, I know we are close, and Zayante, my pal who may be dying in my hands, may still have a chance.

As we come to the final gate above the vet check, we know Jane has alerted people, because a car is driving up to meet us. We pray a vet is going to spring out of that car holding a drug-filled syringe. But it is only Susan, another friend of Zayante's; she cannot help Zayante.

Frantically we yell to her, "We need a vet!"

Susan runs up to take Zay off my exhausted hands and walk him down to the vet check, but I shake my head and keep trotting him past her, yelling, "I can't let him go, he'll go down!"

Susan immediately sees, from the strain on our faces and the pain in Zayante's eyes, and Hiromi exhaustedly running beside, how terribly serious this is, and she jumps back in her car and races down to the vet check, clearing the way, hollering out her window for a veterinarian.

As we ride the final yards down the hill, it's as if Zayante sees help but just can't make it another step; he is trying hard to collapse at our fast trot. I am snarling at him and jerking on him; Gretchen is yelling at Zayante, and screaming for a vet; Hiromi is yelling at him and smacking him to keep him on his feet.

"WE NEED A VET!" I bellow.

I see lots of people and horses down below; I see Susan yelling for a vet; I see some people pointing to the bridge; as we get closer, I see hands pointing the way, hear directions yelled, "Take him over the bridge!"

I hand Zayante off to Hiromi who, without missing a step, runs with him across the bridge to the vet. I jump off Raffiq and follow, as does Gretchen on Spice. Half a dozen people descend upon Zayante and try to unsaddle him, even as he tries to collapse. Kevin the vet is running toward him with a vial in one hand, syringe in other hand, and needle cover in his mouth.

People are now holding Zayante's back end up—two people, four people, as others work to pull his saddle off. Susan immediately yanks him forward as the lifters heave him onto his feet.

I stare, helpless to do any more, as Susan tries to keep Zayante moving along as he still staggers, fighting to not go down. More hands jump in to keep him up and moving, eight hands, twelve hands, holding up his hind end. He's sitting on peoples' knees, everybody wanting to help him.

Zayante's four legs buckle; I think—*he's down this time,* but the human hands lift and heave, literally hold his body up. He is drenched in pain, eyes glazed and stunned, but the humans will not let this horse give up. His body tries to quit, but Zayante is fighting that final defeat with every last ounce of strength, fighting forward like he's always done, looking for that extra mile.

As the shots from the vet start to take effect, Zayante staggers to a momentary stupefied exhausted stop, and I walk up to him.

"Hey, buddy," I say, tears pouring down my face, "hang in there, buddy," rubbing his head, but he is glassy-eyed and does not hear me.

Raffiq stands and watches his buddy Zay, while eating a few bites of grass, and I tell him, "Zay is going to stay here and rest a while; he's tired," and I tell Raffiq now what a terrifically good boy he was for bringing in his uncle Zay in, and I hug him, apologizing for how I treated him on the ride in.

Gretchen and I go on to finish ride—with dozens of people jumping in to help Zayante, we have done what we can and are no longer needed. As we ride away, the drugs are having more of an effect on Zay; the terrible pain is gone, at least temporarily.

I don't know if I will see Zayante alive again; but my mind still cannot accept that this happened. Nor will I let myself think of Nick and Judy riding into that vet check and seeing Zayante. It will hit Nick as hard as it did me.

After we finish the ride, we wait at base camp, sucking up news on Zayante from anybody who has come in from the vet check: many liters of fluid hung on him, he's resting comfortably, he's eating a bit now, he may be taken up to Great Basin vet clinic in Gardnerville. Then the trailer arrives at Ridecamp carrying him, and Zayante backs out of it bellowing for his friends, his head up, eyes bright. There is Hiromi still standing by his side, holding him while people crowd around to have a look at this miracle that we were afraid might not happen. He is led back to his trailer and his other best friend Ross, where a swarm of people attend Zayante like slaves waiting on a king—fresh water, clean blanket, stethoscopes on his sides; and he acts and nibbles like a normal horse.

Optimism is cautious but high—until another hour passes and more of the drugs wear off. I see Zayante no longer eating but standing listlessly, his head hanging lower, his eye not so bright; and that sinking feeling in my gut, that ripping of my heart, returns. Nick is going to haul him and Jackie and Hiromi to the vet clinic. People scurry around to get things ready, and I slip up to Zayante, where Hiromi is still standing by his side. There are tears in her eyes now; she knows this is not over yet. I hug her and tell her she did a great job and she did everything right; but we still won't know the ultimate outcome of this for a while—it will be a long night.

I then step over to Zayante's other side. I will not cry for him, because I still refuse to believe my friend might die.

"Keep hanging in there, buddy, I'll see you when you get back." I pet his neck; I put my arms around his neck and hug him. He hears me this time but he is dull.

Zayante is loaded in the trailer, while Jackie and Hiromi shed tears; I still will not think about anything other than Zayante will be all right.

Zayante pulled through at the vet clinic, without surgery. He eventually returned to light trail riding, but never did another endurance ride, retiring with 13,200 endurance miles—still sixth on the all-time mileage list as of 2013. He lived with his herd until his best buddy Ross died in January 2011. He then went to live with Nick and Judy in the Bay Area, where he was treated like a king, until he died in November of 2013.

Chapter 18—New Zealand

Everything in the house speaks Horse: beat-up cowboy hats hanging on every hook, many pairs of boots by the door caked with various depths of mud, hanging oilskin dusters. A trail of hay on the floor. A bridle on the table that needs repair. A couple of saddle pads that haven't quite made it to the washing machine yet. A lead rope coiled up on the kitchen cabinet.

Jars of tea and coffee, staples of Kiwi life, and two cups by the electric kettle on the stove. Kitchen table bare (but for the bridle), cupboards closed, two bowls and two spoons in the dish drainer—not much time to eat a big breakfast around here.

Stacks of horse magazines cover every flat surface in the living room. Old horse paintings decorate the walls. And there is a single photograph in the house: a Rider of Rohan on his horse. This is Lord of the Rings country, after all.

The rider in Rohirrim battle gear is Trevor, and the horse in battle armor is Picksy. When the call for *Lord of the Rings* extras went out, Trevor took his barely-broke Arabian, who'd had a total of four rides on him, to the *Lord of the Rings* set for three days.

"It was brilliant!" Trevor says. "I went for three days and stayed for three months!"

Trevor really didn't care that it was a series of movies that would end up being New Zealand's biggest production ever, or that he'd be working with some famous actors and a famous director. He and his horse just went to participate, and they had a great time. For Trevor, every new adventure for a horse is a learning experience. Trevor has still never watched the movie. He's in the documentary about the film and he hasn't seen that either. He doesn't even know the names of the actors he worked with. "Blokes" he calls them, not being snide.

It's the horses that matter, and Picksy whom he's most proud of.

"He took everything that was thrown at him," says Trevor. "Standing still while horses galloped straight at him and past him, standing still on a mark for four-and-a-half hours while all kinds of stuff went on around him. Carrying a huge whipping flag when no other horses would get near it, galloping in a line of two hundred horses, no kicking, no bucking; he didn't do anything wrong!

"The makeup people would have to keep passing through the piles of horses to touch up the makeup and costumes, and most of them were a little intimidated, not knowing horses, so I'd take them on little rides when I had free time, to get them used to horses.

"Whenever the director would say, 'Rolling! Three—Two . . .' Picksy and the other horses would perk up and inflate for the cameras . . . then 'One—action' and all this crazy stuff would happen; and when the director said 'Cut!' the horses would let down and relax till the next shot."

I grill Trevor for more details on *Lord of the Rings*, since I'm a fanatic, and I find out he got to be one of the Black Riders; he got to fight Orcs; and he got to do many horse and battle scenes, as did Picksy. Trevor got to die, "once or twice", and he was one of the Rohirrim when they surrounded "that guy" (Aragorn) and "the wee little dwarf" (Gimli) and "the blond guy that shot the arrows" (Legolas). Trevor was once right in the thick of the filming when he held Eomer's spear. In the scene where the Rohirrim galloped up to and surrounded the three heroes, Trevor says, "The wee Dwarf was scared when I galloped down to him and skidded to a stop right in front of him, because my horse's bit broke and was hanging out of his mouth. We did another couple of takes, and I stopped my horse by his breast collar each time, and the wee Dwarf was so startled by the bit hanging out of my horse's mouth that he couldn't concentrate on his lines." Trevor laughs at the memory—it's all about the horses and the riding.

Trevor's porch looks out over his paddocks and toward a distant peak. It's a place to kick your shoes off after a long day's work, and it's where the neighboring farmers like to sit and have a cold beer. They are always popping in on Trevor. The old guys seem to like him and listen to and respect what he has to say. They talk sheep and cows, but Trevor inevitably turns the conversations to horses. The neighbors don't mind, because they have a knowledgeable thing or two to say on the subject, and Trevor often asks their opinions, and he listens closely to what they have to share.

It's very peaceful and silent, but for an occasional horse snort. If you listen *really hard,* you can barely hear distant traffic—probably the odd neighbor driving his tractor home. Trevor grouses at the unnatural noise.

"I'm going to have to move further out into the country!"

The farm has been in his family for four generations. We ride an ATV from paddock to paddock checking out the stock, up and down hills, horses here, cattle there, deer there, the different species mixing and running together at will. One of his stallions likes to hang out in the middle of a mob of deer, and he'll play with them. The deer are raised for meat, though the market is down right now. The market for sheep is even worse. The only thing the wool is good for is keeping the sheep warm in the winter.

But anyway, it's all about the horses. Trevor can't tell you the exact number he has on his three hundred acres, but he can tell you about every one. He knows their breeding backward and forward. He likes to break all his own horses in, too. He likes the challenge of the problem ones. Trevor promises me that he'll break one for me one day.

"In one day?" I ask incredulously.

"Ah, well, maybe not a day. A few hours maybe."

I don't think he's bragging—I think that's just how he does it.

He gleams with fervor when he talks of his horses. He doesn't miss a thing, his eyes intimately caressing each one. He watches their movements, studies their eyes. He's in love. There's something magnetic about him. His horses like him. They go out of their way to come up and see him, even the ones that are not broke. They seem to want to show off for him, ripping up and down the paddocks, swirling around us, showing off who's the fastest and the bravest, racing back and forth, again and again, stopping to turn and look at Trevor for his approval.

Then there's Picksy, former *Lord of the Rings* horse—an equine movie star extra, now an endurance horse and one of Trevor's best pals.

And I am going to ride him.

We mount our steeds and head for the distant mountain.

A steady climb leads us toward the peak. We trot our way up the dirt road, leaving it for a grassy slope. And there we turn our eager horses loose. They attack the hill at a gallop. We climb higher and higher, the hill becomes a mountain, and still we fly upward.

I urge my *Lord of the Rings* horse on. His powerful strides gouge the mountainside. Trevor is leaning forward over his horse's shoulders. They have a length lead over us. I lean over Picksy's neck and smooch in his ears.

The cool wind blasts us in the face, lobbing big floating thistle seeds our way like storm-blown snowflakes. The mane of my Middle Earth horse obscures my view, as the horses leap and launch their way up this steep mountainside. A howl reaches my ears. Trevor looks back at me with a big grin. Picksy and I are gaining on them and I howl back and urge my mount, "Faster!" My breath flows in rhythm with my horse's hoof beats. We pull even with Trevor and the bay, matching strides, surging muscles, churning legs throwing chunks of Middle Earth skyward as we launch forward and upward toward the pinnacle.

I thrust my head into the mane of my mighty steed, and urge him even faster as we race by Mordor, sprint through Gondor and Rohan, race through the Shire and past the Grey Havens where we soar over the Sundering Sea. We outrun the Black Riders and outride the Rohirrim. We run circles around the Orcs and dance past the Uruk-Hai. We duck from spears and dodge arrows and we outfly the Nazgul. We even outdistance the great Shadowfax, Lord of All Horses, who is known to run faster than the wind.

We crest the mountaintop, and come back down to earth beside my friend and his bay horse. Our horses slow to a walk, huffing and puffing.

We have a view spread before us of the entire south of Middle Earth—the south of the South Island of New Zealand, and the Tasman sea, a slice of deep indigo on the horizon beyond.

The wind is howling and cool, as we jump off to lead our horses down the mountain.

Our Kiwi shadows point the way home.

Chapter 19—New Zealand

BEACHIN' IT

"I'm taking you to the most beautiful beach in the world to ride on!"

Trevor is riding his *Lord of the Rings* horse; I climb aboard a strapping Anglo-Arabian. Fritz must be 16.2 hands, strong and athletic. We've brought the horses here for fun, to have a break from their regular work of endurance training and jumping. Trevor and I are here for pure bliss.

We ride onto the sand toward the water and turn into the strong salty Tasman Sea breeze. There are many people and cars on the beach; dogs too, and two large kites flapping in the wind. There are motorbikes and a couple of bicycles. Most everybody we pass waves at us. Can they see how stupidly thrilled I am to be here? I have always dreamed of riding on the beach.

We walk the horses a half mile before we pass the last of the cars. The horses are already relaxed, strolling along, sightseeing like us humans, and obviously enjoying this vacation from their routine.

And then, for miles and miles this place on the planet is ours alone—two people, two horses, and the most beautiful beach in the world. We pick up a trot—a nice big floating trot for Fritz, then a canter—a big rocking chair canter, which quickly turns into a gallop, and then—a flat out run—yikes!

I am still not always instantly completely confident on a galloping horse, because I rarely get to gallop. Nor am I ever totally sure of the new horse I'm getting on. There's always a different saddle to quickly become familiarized with, and each horse has a different way of moving and traveling and responding that you must quickly adjust to. Some horses are stumblers. Some are spooky. Sometimes it takes you a while to sort each other out. But sometimes you just have to quit worrying and let go.

On Fritz, running forty miles per hour down this New Zealand beach, I let go. He somehow makes me feel safe from the start—big strides, big feet, which he places perfectly and smoothly. I feel he isn't going to trip, and he seems like he doesn't bother much with spooking. Only for the first mile or two do I think about being a bit nervous—we are going so *fast*—and then the feeling is gone. I trust Trevor, who is riding beside me, and who would not put me on a scary horse. I trust Fritz.

I balance just right over his withers, sitting motionless as we pound down the beach. The strong headwind is *hammering* us in the face and the noise is deafening. We're not asking our horses to race each other; they are just doing it. They're sprinting down this empty beach with abandon and delight, ears flattened against their necks, eyeballing each other, pounding along the surf, our tracks now the only evidence of our passage, denting the sand for miles. Tears are pouring out of my eyes from the chilly wind.

Picksy pins his ears harder and runs faster, and behind him Fritz digs in and rips along right after him. It's such a rush! Here I am, in New Zealand, sprinting down an empty beach (alongside a *Lord of the Rings* horse!), with nobody but the gulls to watch us tear by, nobody to see me grinning like a dope—until Trevor looks over at me, beaming just as big.

The eleven kilometers zip by in too short a time, and we slow down to turn into the high grassy dunes through an almost hidden passage. It leads to a track through the beach bush, which leads to . . .

A surprise forest! Thick groves of tall cedar and pine trees swallow us, a dense canopy shielding us from the wind, a layer of pine needles carpeting our path and muffling our hoof beats, smart little trails twisting through the darkened woods. We trot along the narrow paths, break into a canter along the wider ones, leap to a gallop on the straights, the horses thundering along as if they know all the secret passages.

Sometimes small tree branches hang over the trail, and as we zip under them, Fritz ducks his head and I drop onto his neck and duck with him, but we don't slow down, not a fraction, not even when, at one spot, the tree branches squeeze us on both sides and from on top! I throw myself flat on Fritz's neck and shut my eyes tight, as he ducks and blasts through. The branches rake my back.

"Yee haw!"

Our horses are having a ball, Picksy leading the way with his tail up, Fritz chasing him merrily. Fritz and I are thinking as one. He switches leads at the canter as I think them around the turns; he slows around the corners and launches back into a gallop when the trail straightens out, even as I move with him. We turn left and right and backward and forward. It's a game, trotting here, galloping there; horse ears pricked forward, always looking for the next bend in the trail. Fritz never misses a beat, never stumbles, never puts a foot wrong. He's very athletic and balanced. When we come to tricky roots across the trail, he doesn't slow down a bit but he seems to put an extra step in there to feel them out and travel over them smoothly.

We eventually pop back out on the beach for our eleven kilometers back along the water, the horses still full of spunk and spirit. We are still not asking them to move out; they are doing it because they can—trotting, cantering, sprinting, running flat out again, a breathless race for fun down the beach. Going this direction, with the strong wind at our backs, we have no wind at all, so it is silent but for the thumping of eight hooves in the sand. The sound is so perfect I don't say anything, just listen, and grin madly. Trevor is doing the same. He never gets tired of coming here.

We fly above the water line, Fritz digging in to keep up with Picksy, Picksy playfully spooking at the water rolling up at us. Trevor aims for the water and we follow, Picksy's heels kicking up ocean and sand in Fritz's and my faces.

My gray gelding carries me gallantly, on the most perfect ride, on the most beautiful beach in the world.

Chapter 20—Idaho

WANNA BE A COWGIRL

A bull was on the loose.

It belonged to a local rancher named Rawl (what a perfect name for a cowboy), who drove up with a horse and trailer to round up the errant beast and haul him home. The bull had meandered his way down from the Owyhee Mountains like he did every fall, but he found himself on our upper two hundred acres and he decided that he liked it. He had been hanging out up there and enjoying our grass the last couple of days, and felt no urge to move further homeward.

Knowing a little bit about cattle and ranching, Steph and I thought we'd help Rawl out, so she saddled up her fast endurance horse, Rhett, and I saddled up the ol' ranch-horse-turned-endurance horse, Rushcreek Mac (originally from the famed Rush Creek Land and Livestock Company in Nebraska), and we set off up the canyon with Rawl on his cow horse Rusty, and Rawl's three cow dogs.

Now I thought Mac could trot, and I knew Rhett could move fast, but Rusty the cow horse on a mission had a working business trot that put our endurance horses to shame. Rusty's cow horse shuffle left us cantering in his dust just to catch up with him. As we'd mounted our horses, Rawl had made some joke about his old horse and his old cow dogs and his old self riding and keeping up with some younger women, but after the first five acres were covered, it was easy to see who would outpace whom when it came down to . . . Bull.

The plan was to drive the bull back down to the house where Rawl had pulled his trailer into our lower paddock. We'd run the bull into a pen, and Rawl would back his trailer up to the gate and load him up. Easy, right? Especially with three real cow dogs, two real ranch horses, and one fast endurance horse on the job, plus a cowboy, and two experienced endurance-riding horse women who could ride all day and who knew a bit about cowboying.

We spotted the bull halfway up the canyon, and rode past him far enough, then turned back and headed straight for him. The bull turned to face us, coming quickly to terms with the fact that his lazy days of solitary grazing in his new kingdom were over, and then he whipped around and took off like a jackrabbit with his ears lit on fire alongside the crick, bulling his way through the tall sagebrush.

Rusty was off like a shot behind him, and Mac and I were off like a ricocheting bullet in a metal tube after him. I don't have any idea what Steph and Rhett were doing, because I was just trying to hang on. The faster we went—and it was getting faster and faster—the more excited Mac got, trying to yank the reins out of my hands, and throwing his head straight up in the air—and therefore not watching the rough ground we were covering.

Rusty must have been floating above the ground because he kept putting more distance between us, while Mac was dodging this way and that through the sagebrush, over downed logs, leaping like a gazelle three feet in the air over one sage (it's possible Mac may have leapt two feet, and I came out of the saddle a foot). I quit trying to guide Mac because his steering and my steering were not harmonizing, and this was going much too fast and I didn't really know how to proceed. I just let Mac have the reins while I concentrated on holding on. I'd brought my camera because I thought I'd be taking pictures and documenting the whole thing—HA!

The bull tried to lose us by diving into the middle of the dry crick—which was very rocky with difficult footing and overgrown bushes; and Rusty and Rawl without any hesitation plunged right after him.

Steph, behind me, yelled, "I'm getting out of the crick!" while I was a step ahead of her, already pointing Mac out of the brushy maze.

Steph headed to the right bank. Mac and I took the left, and we stayed a bit behind the commotion down there. It was part of our strategy, you see—we were going to help keep the bull moving forward and not let him leap up and over the twenty-foot high bank on the left side of the crick and double back on us. In reality, there was no way on God's Green Earth I would have tried bushwhacking with Mac after them through the jungle of thick willows and downed branches and walls of tumbleweeds and logs and tripping rocks and monsters that were down there.

As it was, it was pretty excitingly alarming up top, because the bull below us was making a ginormously scary racket crashing through the brush in the crick; the three snarling barking frenzied cow dogs were attacking the bull's heels; Rawl was yelling at the dogs to back off; and Rusty was just bulling his way along right after the whole shebang, oblivious to the terror.

Mac and I couldn't see any live creatures below us, but the brush and willows were swaying and swirling back and forth in a frightening sort of way, and what with all the hysterical barking and yelling, it sounded as if bodies were being ripped apart. Beneath me, Mac the cow horse was either soooooo excited about finally getting back to working his beloved cows, or he was thinking, *'Be-Geeez-Us! Horses and cows and dogs never got ripped apart and eaten in Nebraska!'* because he was absolutely freaking out. I had to keep both hands on the steering wheel, and hope I wasn't going to get tossed down into the bull-and-monster threshing machine below.

Despite the predicament I was in—not knowing if I was going to get dumped off my horse (then laughed at—"She can ride a hundred miles but she can't stay on a *cow horse* when a *cow* is around!"), I think I still had it easier than Steph on Rhett, who, across the crick, was *really* losing it. Rhett is *not* a cow horse, does not *want* to be a cow horse, and thinks cows should not even exist on the planet. Rhett and Steph were spinning and lunging and climbing in the air and galloping back and forth sideways instead of forward—from what I could see on my glimpses of them anyway, as I had plenty of my own problems to keep myself occupied. Mac was cantering in place, throwing his head down, throwing it up and back into my lap (I was really afraid I'd get smacked in the face and knocked off his back), snorting, trying to wheel—I wasn't quite sure what he was going to do, and I wasn't sure if he was planning to do it with me or not.

Finally, the cow dogs laid off the bull, the bull chose to come out of the crick and continue moving down-canyon faster on more hospitable ground, and I was able to let Mac move forward instead of up and down. He was still terribly excited, but fortunately, he was somewhat controllable. Rawl and Rusty stayed on the bull's tail, and Mac and I hung way back and to the side—you know, in case he might have doubled back . . . which was highly unlikely, and in which case we might have turned tail and run anyway.

Steph and Rhett crossed the crick and caught up with me and my dancing horse, and the one word she uttered was something like "#*+&%@^!!" and that about summed it up for me and Mac too! Rhett's head was high in the air like a giraffe and his eyes were big as pie plates, and he and Mac snorted back and forth hard and loudly like wild deer do when they're facing down a death threat.

"SNOORRRTT (Did you see that **BULL!?**)"

"SNOORRRTT (Did **YOU** see that bull!?)"

"SNOORRRTT (Did you **SEE** that bull!?)"

The bull made his way to and through the gate like he knew what he was doing, and on down to the pens at the house. He might have gone right on into his awaiting pen—but then our cow-senseless dogs ran out thinking they'd help. The bull tried to make a break for the crick; I moved Mac to join Rawl and Rusty to keep the bull from crossing it or running past it and down the fence, otherwise we'd have had a heap of trouble getting him back. Rawl and Rusty blocked the crick crossing, and the big 1900-pound bull turned toward me and Mac and the fence line, and he started coming at us.

Uh oh.

Did I mention the bull was big?

I didn't know if Mac would face him down, but I sure didn't want to fall off my horse right in front of this oncoming bull, so unthinkingly (no time to think!) I sent Mac right at the fence to block him and call his bluff and turn him, and at the last second I about chickened out and leaped over the fence without my horse, because the bull sure didn't act like he was stopping.

But Mac knew what he was doing and he was no longer afraid o' no bull. He stopped the bull, and we stood there in a face-off. Rawl and I and our horses held the bull there a minute and let him settle down before driving him back around the corner, where he went right on into the waiting pen.

As Rawl backed his trailer up, shooed the bull right inside, and shut the door on him, we tied our horses up. Rusty was already snoozing under the barn roof. Mac stood and acted like he'd had everything under control the whole time, while Rhett danced back and forth around the hitching post, his eyes still bugged out and veins poking out like flood-stage rivers under his skin.

I'd done a wee bit of cattle herding before, so I thought I knew what today's bull drive would be all about—it was only one bull, after all; and I thought I was riding a real cow horse, but either Mac had forgotten all about his cow horse days, or they rushed back to him too fast, or, I just didn't know how to ride a cow horse after all.

I decided to stick to endurance riding—I don't wanna be a Cowgirl anymore.

Chapter 21—France

JE SUIS PERDU

I am lost.

I know about ten words in French, three of which might come in handy at some point: *Je suis perdu*—I am lost.

Nicky hauls me and Dougal a couple of miles from home and drops us off. She calls Dougal "God's Horse." Her husband Richard calls him "the King of All Horses." He is a fine looking equine, although I can't quite imagine what they mean.

Nicky points the general direction home—through the woods, over a forested ridge, down through the other little valley, and toward the tiny village of Gesvres. I don't have a phone. I don't have a map. Other than Gesvres, the closest I can describe my location, if I must, is "northwest France," and I sure can't explain any of it in French.

And Nicky leaves us, driving away with a wave and a grin, saying, "Dougal knows the way home."

We start out riding along a two-track beside a pasture of cows, who turn to follow us; and Dougal trots to leave them behind. We come to a split in the road. Both have old signs that say La Propriété Privée and both lead into the forest—but there is nowhere else to go.

Without pause, Dougal chooses the right fork. It is little used, a narrow single lane covered with leaves—and it is a bridle path, local routes that villagers used in historic times, now called Right of Ways.

Some of the trees have two horizontal pink stripes, and the number five. They lead somewhere . . . but I do not know where I am going.

I thought I could rely on the compass in my head, because it works fairly well when I pay attention to my surroundings—but this is the forest, where I can't see far through the trees, and our track has been gradually curving—but I can't tell how much. There are now dark clouds above so there is no sunlight with which to determine the direction, and I soon lose all sense of orientation.

But Dougal moves forward without hesitation. He turns at some forks in the trail, goes straight past others. Sometimes we are following pink striped tree trunks; sometimes we are not on bridle paths at all.

At one trail junction—when I am sure we are heading straight toward home, Dougal turns away on a path to the right. I feel as if we are going opposite of where we should be headed, but Dougal is absolutely sure of where he is going. I don't try to put my two cents worth in. He picks up a canter, ears pricked forward, and we float along swiftly through the forest, his bare feet falling softly on the grassy track. Perhaps we are getting further away from home, and he just likes to canter this stretch in this direction. Perhaps we are heading straight toward our village. I have absolutely no idea.

The forest is mostly silent—birds are rare and there's no sign of anything or anyone else. We zig then zag, follow a curving track, make a few more turns in this green maze. We cross a paved road, but there are no houses, no cars, no people of whom I might ask the way, if I could even make myself understood. I can't even properly pronounce the name of our village; it falls out mangled off my tongue. No matter. Dougal saunters along, snacking on chestnut leaves hanging over the trail.

And then we emerge onto another small road—and I recognize where we are—at a paddock where Dougal has spent time babysitting a couple of young colts. I know the way to our village now. The King of All Horses has brought me homeward.

Je ne suis pas perdu—I am not lost!

Chapter 22—Idaho

MY KINDRED SPIRIT

DARK STORM CLOUDS HAVE GATHERED OVER THE OWYHEE MOUNTAINS AND LIE DIRECTLY BETWEEN US AND HOME, SIX MILES AWAY. I AM INCAPABLE OF HEARING THUNDER UNLESS IT'S RIGHT ON TOP OF ME, AND THOSE CLOUDS LOOK A BIT SUSPICIOUS . . . AND DANGEROUS. I AM STARTING TO GET NERVOUS. WE'VE BEEN TROTTING STEADILY DOWN THE TRAIL, BUT NOW WE PICK UP THE PACE, TROTTING AND CANTERING, FAST, FOR FIVE MILES WITHOUT STOPPING.

I AM HALF SCARED AND HALF ENCHANTED BY THIS STORM. JOSE AND I ARE HURTLING DOWN THE ROAD, HEADING STRAIGHT INTO THE BLACK WALL OF LOW, MENACING CLOUDS. WE ARE INTENT UPON GETTING TO THE BATES CREEK RIM, DOWN OFF THIS FLAT, AND OUT OF THIS STORM CLOUD WE ARE STARING DOWN.

I MARVEL AT JOSE'S LIMITLESS STRENGTH—HIS HUNDREDTH MILE IS LIKE HIS FIRST MILE IN THIS TWO-DAY ENDURANCE RIDE. I CANNOT BELIEVE THIS HORSE IS STILL MOVING SO EAGERLY AND EASILY. A FEW SPATTERING DROPS PRESAGE THE STORM BEFORE RAIN DRENCHES THE DESERT, SAND AND SAGE, HORSES AND RIDERS. I SQUINT MY EYES, AND JOSE BOWS HIS HEAD AGAINST THE SPITTING RAINDROPS, BUT DOES NOT HESITATE NOR SKIP A BEAT, AS WE SOAR INTO THE BLACK CLOUD. MY HORSE FLIES WITHOUT WINGS. HIS HOOVES LIGHTLY SKIM THE EARTH. HE SWIFTLY MOVES UNFALTERINGLY FORWARD, NOT IN A RACE TO GET HOME, BUT TO DANCE IN THE OWYHEE STORM.

It wasn't love at first ride. He was a stumbler; and a tripping horse leaves you feeling quite insecure in the saddle. He was only four at the time, and I didn't know if it was because he was young or just innately clumsy, or just hadn't had enough wet saddle pads.

I'd ridden Jose on a visit to Idaho, where friends had taken me on one of the most scenic rides of their myriad backyard BLM trails. I still remember the first breathtaking, addicting views of the dramatic Owyhee desert country from that knife ridge trail above the yawning Little Hart Creek Canyon—that and Jose's stumbling.

Two years later, I'd followed another of those serendipitous horse paths and moved to that Owyhee country in Idaho, to start work for those same friends, Steph and John of www.Endurance.net, as a photographing, writing, traveling reporter and horse rider. Jose was one of the many endurance horses I regularly rode and conditioned for Steph. He'd gotten over his stumbling by then, but he wasn't my favorite horse to ride. When Jose started his first season of 50-mile rides that year as a six-year-old, when I got a chance to endurance ride I always sat in someone else's saddle . . . but by the end of that year, Jose had become my horse of choice on training rides.

It only escalated from there. By the next year, that horse had, without my being aware of how it had happened, wormed his way under my skin—like one of those old friends you'd been around for a while, when out of the darkness the spotlight flashes on and lights him up center stage, and you suddenly realized he was awfully special, and you started noticing all those unique qualities he possessed, and you wondered how you hadn't noticed them before.

When you're eyeballing him, physically, Jose's not a spectacular equine specimen to look at. Especially sans saddle, he wouldn't win any equine beauty contest. He's a plain, medium-sized light bay with two white socks and a star, and a very swayed back—a strange phenomenon that happened over one summer, though it never has bothered him physically. He could easily pass for some old nag, but I would never say that to his face.

But when your eyes meet his, that's what distinguishes him from the rest. His are knowing eyes, astute, calculating, capable of sizing you up. Those eloquent eyes peered down into my soul and tangled and became one with my heartstrings before I knew what was happening. When I look at Jose, I see pure beauty, outside and inside. *That* I will tell him to his face, and have.

I'd never been around such an extremely perceptive and intelligent horse before. There was always something special going on between those soft brown ears of his. He was particularly observant: always the first horse to see a human walking around outside, or the speck of a cow far away on a hill. He noticed when I was gone on a trip, and he was the first horse to walk up and greet me when I returned.

He was curious about things and often seemed to study what I was doing, filing it away for future reference. It didn't take him long to figure out how to untie his lead rope from the hitching rail. One of his herd-mates, Dudley, was known for his Escape Artist talents, and Jose picked up some methods from him, learning how to open certain gates, learning how and when to slip through a hot-wired fence on the day it wasn't hot.

Jose always left the hay or herd to come visit when I walked into the paddock. He always seemed to listen when I talked to him, and so I began talking to him like I did human beings. He looked me in the eye when I spoke, and I swear he understood everything I said.

One day disaster struck one of the herd: something happened up the canyon (which we humans never figured out) where one mare got tangled up in a barbed wire fence and nearly cut her hind leg off. Jose somehow ended up on the *opposite* side of the four-strand fence, but without a scratch on him. My heart stopped when I first saw him separated across the fence from the herd, but when I saw he was unscathed, and I grabbed and hugged his neck, weeping in relief, he nudged me as if to say, *I'm all right, silly!* Somehow, he'd carefully crossed that barbed wire fence without hurting himself, and he was smart enough to stay there and not hurt himself trying to get back to the herd.

He was extraordinarily cognizant of his surroundings, and he shared my love of exploring new trails. There's something magical about laying footsteps or hoof prints over new ground, and I swear he appreciated new scenery in this desert country of hidden canyons as much as I did. We both wondered where that new trail went, or what was around that fold in the hills that we'd never checked out before.

On rides, Jose loved to stop on the top of hills and look around, his gaze sweeping slowly back and forth at the landscape around and below, or the wildlife in the distance, taking it all in. He wasn't nervous or anxious. He was looking. Assimilating. Studying. *Contemplating.* The minute muscles over his nostrils quivered, the synapses in his brain fired and spun around and absorbed the details. His ears swiveled back and forth, picking up sounds present and past. I could feel the cogs turning in his brain, and the feelings swirling in his soul. He'd stand stock-still for five minutes on a ridge, just observing and thinking. I called him The Deep Thinker.

Jose had Elf Eyes—he could see further and better than any human. Even while sure-footedly trotting along a trail, he'd notice a tiny pertinent dot in the distance—a moving truck on the highway, a camouflaged coyote among the sagebrush, a raven flying low in the sky, a string of antelope bounding over a hill. I learned to look for what he was watching, because it was always something interesting.

Best of all, Jose was utterly sensible and bold on the trails. He was afraid of . . . nothing. If we did ride upon something odd, say a funny-looking sagebrush that had been newly trampled by a cow to look like a Horse Eating Monster, if he hesitated, I'd let him stop and look at it. I'd explain exactly what it was (since he understood what I said), letting him figure it out and reconstruct in his brain the original standing sagebrush. He'd never have a problem with it again.

I did fall off of him one time: a balloon got us. We'd both seen the deflated helium balloon ahead of us tangled in a low bush as we were trotting along a wash. We both only gave it a glance; but right as we moved past it, a breeze kicked it up at us. Bad timing. Jose spooked away and I fell off, landing on my back in a sagebrush. My lying upside down in a bush startled him more than the balloon had. I had a hold of his reins, and he stood there looking down at me completely perplexed. I stood up, mounted back up, and on we went with our ride. I know Jose isn't afraid of balloons, but I might slow down a bit the next time we pass one if the wind is blowing!

While Jose was always calm and mellow on the training trails, when we did our first 50-mile endurance ride together in the spring of 2008, I discovered a wonderful secret personality hidden beneath his hide. The endurance horse Jose was strong, keen, competitive, and forward. He was an absolute blast to ride. All business. Bombed down the trail, threw himself wholeheartedly into it. During that ride, at the first vet check, when I walked away from him to go fetch his food, Jose tried to follow me, and then he nickered at me when I returned with his bucket.

That pretty much completely sealed the Jose deal for me.

THE SNEAK ATTACK

A HORSE ROLLING IN THE DIRT IS AS CONTAGIOUS AS A HORSE YAWNING. ONE HORSE DOES IT, THEY ALL HAVE TO DO IT.

JOSE FINDS THE BEST SPOT, BEGINS PAWING IN THE DIRT, DROPS TO HIS FRONT KNEES, COLLAPSES HIS HIND END, AND ROLLS. WIGGLES IN THE DIRT, RUBS HIS HEAD, SCRATCHES HIS HIDE, GRINDS THE DIRT IN.

HE'S GOT KAZAM'S ATTENTION.

JOSE RISES TO HIS FEET, TURNS A HALF CIRCLE, THEN PLUNGES RIGHT BACK TO THE EARTH. SHIMMIES ON ONE SIDE, KICKS HIS FEET IN THE AIR AND ROLLS OVER TO THE OTHER SIDE; SQUIGGLES SOME MORE. HE LEAPS TO HIS FEET AND GIVES A MIGHTY SHAKE; MANE, TAIL, FORELOCK SPEWING DIRT EVERYWHERE. AHHHH, HE SHUDDERS AND SIGHS.

KAZAM WALKS OVER TO THE GREAT ROLL SPOT. JOSE WATCHES HIM. KAZAM SNIFFS, PAWS, TURNS IN CIRCLES TO EXACTLY THE RIGHT COMPASS BEARING, AND DROPS TO THE GROUND. HE WIGGLES ON HIS BACK, POUNDS THE SKY WITH HIS HOOVES, ROLLS ONTO HIS SIDE.

WITH KAZAM'S BACK TO HIM, AND KAZAM'S ATTENTION SOLELY FOCUSED ON HIS GREAT DIRT ROLL, JOSE SNEAKS UP AND BITES KAZAM ON THE BUTT!

JOSE WHEELS ON HIS HIND END AND TAKES OFF IN A SPRINT AS KAZAM SPRINGS UP TO GIVE CHASE! JOSE SLAMS ON HIS BRAKES, REACHES DOWN TO PICK UP AN EMPTY FEED BUCKET, WHIRLS AROUND AND HOLDS IT UP TO KAZAM. KAZAM SKIDS TO A STOP, STICKS HIS HEAD IN THE (EMPTY) BUCKET, AND ABRUPTLY FORGETS HIS ATTACK PLAN.

BATH TIME

IT'S TERRIBLY HOT. WHAT BETTER WAY TO COMBAT THE SUMMER DESERT HEAT THAN TO PLAY IN THE WATER. JOSE STROLLS UP TO THE SPRINKLER, WALKS OVER THE TOP OF IT, THOROUGHLY SOAKING HIS BELLY. HE TURNS TO STAND DIRECTLY IN FRONT OF THE STREAM OF WATER SO IT SHOOTS HIM IN THE CHEST. HE PIVOTS, 360 DEGREES IN ONE DIRECTION, METHODICALLY COVERING HIS BODY, THEN HE TURNS 360 DEGREES IN THE OPPOSITE DIRECTION, GIVING HIMSELF THE PERFECT SHOWER.

SOME IN THE HERD ARE WATCHING HIM. SOME OF THEM WALK OVER TO WATCH, TRY TO FIGURE OUT HOW IT'S DONE.

JOSE FACES THE SPRINKLER AGAIN, POSITIONS HIMSELF SO IT SHOOTS HIM UNDER THE JAW NEXT TIME IT COMES AROUND. SATISFIED HE'S WET ENOUGH, HE HEADS OFF TO ROLL IN THE DIRT.

THE OTHERS IN THE HERD DON'T QUITE HAVE THE UNIQUE BATHING TECHNIQUE DOWN, BUT SOME HAVE FIGURED OUT THAT IF THEY STAND IN ONE SPOT, THE ROTATING SPRINKLER WILL EVENTUALLY COME AROUND AND SPRINKLE THEIR HIDES.

THE PADDOCK BECOMES A GIANT DUST CLOUD, AS THE DOZEN HORSES ROLL AND WIGGLE THEIR WAY AROUND THE GREAT ROLL SPOTS.

If his intelligence was off the charts, his talent for play was genius.

I'd never been around such a frolicsome horse before. Horseplay took on a whole new meaning when the Owyhee Social Director was at work. Jose could coerce every member of the herd into playing. Whether or not they were the player types before they met Jose, he eventually wore them down. Jose knew just how far to push each horse: some had a hair-trigger play gene, and other horses, like the solemn Rhett, had none, though Jose still got Rhett to head wrestle, when nobody was looking.

Horseplay 101 started with the Head Wrestling: nipping with bared teeth, jabbing at each other, feinting in and darting away. Sometimes hides got ripped until horses honed their dodging reflexes, but that never discouraged them from going at it. Jose directed some horses to Nose Wrestle: noses pressed together as if locked in a kiss.

Bite My Leg was the next tactic: reaching down to try and grab another horse's leg, while spinning and ducking out of the way to keep his own legs safe.

A spinoff of Bite My Leg was The Strike. A lightning fast thrust of a foreleg at a ninety-degree angle to the body gave the partner a chance to dance out of the way while trying to bite the offending foreleg.

Some of the herd learned to play Tug-Of-War. Any old stick or sagebrush branch would do, and if his partner didn't catch on to grab the stick, Jose would bonk him on the head with it.

The most rambunctious horses progressed to Tallest Horse. Sometimes they'd rear so high and clash that they'd nearly shove the other over backwards. Sometimes they'd land on top of each other, a *pas de deux* of balletic dance gone askew.

Some of the horses could skillfully combine all Jose's games into serious-looking mock battles: Bite-Spin-Chase-Sprint-Kick-Strike-Rear-Clash-Retreat-Attack. Some days Jose incited the whole herd into motion—a fluid choreographed school-of-fish tango of horses ebulliently running, leaping, and spinning, with tossing heads, flying manes, flipping tails. It was a glorious spectacle to behold.

Jose even got my older horse Stormy to romp around with him a few times, something I was astonished by, as I'd never seen Stormy frolic with any other horses, anywhere, ever. I'd thought Stormy was too solemn and dignified to play (or perhaps too lazy), but horsing around with Jose made him look *more* dignified.

It was Jose who converted a characterless Rushcreek Mac into a super personality. Bred and born a working ranch horse in Nebraska, cattle work was all Mac had known until he arrived at Steph's endurance ranch in Idaho at age eight. He knew nothing of affection, or of horse treats or carrots or apples—he was a work horse. And he wasn't particularly interested in chumming around with the humans or horses around our place . . . until Jose worked his magic.

Through Jose's devoted persistence, Mac became one of Jose's most ardent roughhouse companions. They played often and hard, chasing, dodging, wrestling, rearing and clashing, and finding toys to play with together. They ripped apart cardboard boxes, removed and lost fly masks, shredded brooms, and ripped up more blankets than I cared to report to their owner. Mac started to appreciate, then demand, horse treats, and attention, too; and it was all because Jose's infectious enthusiasm for life and play bestowed a personality upon Mac.

And even if Jose couldn't stir up anybody in the herd to play with him, he had no trouble entertaining himself. He'd race circles around and diagonals through the herd. He'd stop and paw and try to catch and bite his moving ankle, as if he were trying to nip another horse's pawing leg. Sometimes he'd almost fall down from biting his own ankle and pulling back too hard. He'd buck in mid-gallop, and he'd carom over the earth with all four feet in unison, like a gazelle. He'd lie down to roll, then leap up, spin, and bolt away with style and grace. He could dance solo just as well as in company, a beguiling, cavorting creature full of *joie de vivre* that made my heart laugh.

Long gone was the torpid stumblebum I'd first ridden a few years earlier. From the rough play with his herd mates, Jose had matured into a terrific athlete with phenomenal quickness, balance, and strength, which metamorphosed into extraordinary capability on the endurance trails. Jose had become my dream riding horse.

He was smooth and sure-footed and had a powerful, steady nine to ten mile per hour trot. It felt bottomless. He never seemed to get tired, and he was always ready to cover that next mile. He had enough go; he had enough whoa. He didn't pull my arms out of their sockets for wanting to go faster. He was smart enough to know to slow down over rocky ground and watch his footing. He was constantly alert enough to notice and appreciate his surroundings, even while boogieing down the trail.

He wasn't nervous or spooky, like a lot of Arabians are. He would just as happily follow a horse on trails, or lead the way with his ears enthusiastically pricked forward. Jose gave me confidence—he felt *safe* beneath me. Step after step, mile after mile, Jose simply left me marveling at his seemingly limitless power and willingness.

Never having owned my own endurance horse, I've ridden many different ones over the years. You learn a lot from riding many different horses. But you also learn a lot riding one horse for many, many miles. My pal Jose became only the second horse that I'd ridden to over a thousand AERC miles (Royal Raffiq was the first). You get to know each other pretty well sharing that many miles of trails together. Your communication becomes subtle; minds begin to think alike. The slightest shift of my weight at a fork in a trail had Jose immediately taking that direction. My thought of moving up from a trot to a canter was just that: more of a thought, both of our bodies moving into a canter. Over the years I came to ride him in a sidepull instead of a bit, because we communicated so well and I trusted him so completely.

It was during Jose's ten-year-old season, and my twelfth year of riding endurance, that we completed seven hundred twenty miles together, my highest-mileage season ever. And the highlight of that year was the 5-day Owyhee Canyonlands. I'd ridden a couple of 3-day rides before, and one 4-day ride (on Zayante), but it was my first, and Jose's first, 5-day ride.

I love multi-day endurance rides the best. I love the challenge of managing my horse in a 50-mile ride, day after day, judging the right pace to make him last, keeping him free from injury or blemishes (no sore back, no girth galls, no knocked or bruised legs), keeping him fit and healthy to continue the next day. I love the tiredness I feel at the end of the day, the weariness of climbing in the saddle the next morning, and the miraculous sensation when that fatigue melts away as my horse starts down the next day's trail. I love the feeling of my horse readily and eagerly heading out to do it again.

And I loved the Owyhee Canyonlands ride. It didn't matter that the trails were repeats of the same trails we'd done over the years. I never got tired of the home trails. Neither did Jose. And what mattered most was that every morning, for five days in a row that September, when I stepped into his pen, Jose walked up to me and stuck his nose in his halter, and we saddled up and hit the trails with friends Connie and Phinneas.

Every day, for fifty miles, instead of getting more tired, Jose and I both got stronger and stronger. Every day, every stride, I was awed by the power and enthusiasm emanating from the soul beneath me, through the climbs and descents, the creeks, the sand, the rocks, the heat, and the dust. There were moments, minutes, hours of enlightenment in those miles, where Jose and I were one together: flowing in the same motion and rhythm, being in the same thoughts, harmonizing breaths, synchronizing heartbeats. A perfect state of Zen with a perfect being. Enlightenment.

Jose finished the 250th mile on the last day as strong as he'd started his first mile on day one. And when the veterinarian checked his pulse at the final vet check, it was *forty-four*—just about what it was when he pulsed in for the ride, five days earlier. I hugged my beautiful mount at the end of that ride, buried my tears in his mane, and thanked him for the astounding gift he shared with me. '

Eclipsing that amazing accomplishment, Robert, the ride's head veterinarian, handed out his annual 5-day Best Condition award, to "the horse who, if I was being chased by Indians, I'd want to make my escape on . . . and the award goes to . . . Jose." *Oh my God,* was all I could think, all I could get out of my mouth. I wanted to weep. Jose had done it all just because I asked him to, and he'd done it so effortlessly, so agreeably.

We won a year-end award for our seven hundred twenty miles together, and AERC sent me a vest with my name and Jose's name embroidered on it. I'd never won anything from AERC before or since, but nothing will ever top this vest. When I wear it, I remember our miles and miles of partnership that year: the hundreds of miles of hoof prints and dust kicked up over fabulous country on my best pal; cold mornings, hot days, sun, rain, wind, and thunderstorms together; laughs and tears together; great horse and human friends; windburn, sunburn, tiredness, tirelessness together; a joyous sense of willingness and wildness, of good times, good fortune, and perfection.

HOW DO I PUT INTO WORDS A HORSE LIKE JOSE?

HOW DO I DESCRIBE THIS MAGNIFICENT HORSE, WHOSE SPIRIT HAS FOREVER STOLEN A PIECE OF MY SOUL?

JOSE IS AN AVATAR—TWO HOOVES IN THE HUMAN/HORSE WORLD, TWO HOOVES IN THE SPIRIT WORLD. HE'S AN OLD SOUL, WITH FAR MORE UNDERSTANDING OF THE WORLD THAN I HAVE. WHEN HE GRACIOUSLY CARRIES ME ON HIS BACK, WHEN WE RIDE THE TRAILS TOGETHER, HE SHARES WITH ME HOOF STEPS FROM HIS PAST LIVES, TO SHARE WITH ME IN THIS LIFE, AND TO CARRY ON TO OUR NEXT LIVES. I AM PRIVILEGED, AND PROFOUNDLY BEHOLDEN, TO THIS EXCEPTIONAL BEING WHO GALLOPED INTO MY LIFE. HE IS MORE THAN MY TEACHER, MORE THAN MY FRIEND.

JOSE IS MY KINDRED SPIRIT.

Chapter 23—Idaho

MY LOVE

The belly sags a bit southward now at the age of twenty-two, the force of gravity sharpening the withers and spine further north. The paunch swings a bit like a pendulum as he walks, the taut muscles of an extraordinarily fit athlete having gone soft. The urge to race the wind has faded, though the occasional burst of remembered prowess and glory sends him to the front of the herd in the occasional race down the canyon.

Beneath the older, stretchier hide, I still see the extraordinary beauty and spirit that first grabbed hold of me; and when Stormy turns those dark brown eyes my way and nickers at me, I still melt. My knees get weak, every time, even after all these years. I look at Stormy and think, *I can't believe this stunning creature is my horse.*

Noble blood flows in his veins. Combing through Stormy's pedigree is like running your fingers through antique tassels of the finest silk.

He's a grandson of Mr. Prospector—known for his brilliant speed on the track, and as one of the most influential sires and broodmare sires in Thoroughbred history. Native Dancer—the "Grey Ghost," winner of twenty-one of his twenty-two starts, multiple Champion and Horse of the Year, ancestor of innumerable champions—is both his great-great, and great-great-great grandsire. Northern Dancer—U.S. Champion and Canadian Horse of the Year, and also one of the greatest sires in Thoroughbred history—is a great grandsire.

The magnificent Man O' War—ranked as the top Thoroughbred racehorse of all time in some polls—shows up in his pedigree four times. The Tetrarch, a spotted speedy freak of a horse sometimes called "possibly the greatest two-year-old of all time," from County Kildare, Ireland—where I first galloped racehorses—is sprinkled throughout his pedigree six times.

There are other greats: Ben Brush, Broomstick, Whisk Broom, Domino, St. Simon, Nearco, and Frizette. (But if I start to wax too poetic, there's a mare named Blue Tit in there twice also.)

Stormy had a decent career on the racetrack: five seasons of racing; six wins, nine seconds, and four thirds in forty-two starts; career earnings of $45,882. That translated to Stormy about breaking even with the expense of being a racehorse for his years on the track, something a majority of racehorses do not do for their owners. Most spectacular statistic is that Stormy never had a lameness problem and never got hurt, other than that time he almost bit his tongue off in a race. He still bears that gnarly scar as a visible reminder of his racing history.

He worked hard as a racehorse, made his ancestors proud (whether or not he won stakes races or championship titles), made his groom proud, and came out unscathed on the other side of the racetrack, where he landed with his lucky human. My housemate had been right all along—I had ended up with Stormy, because we were obviously meant to be together.

Our post-racing relationship started out on a shaky foundation of misunderstanding. It revolved around the word "retired".

When I told Stormy he was retired, I naturally meant, "retired from racing".

Stormy clearly thought I meant "retired from everything but eating".

Honest work never hurt a horse. I didn't see why Stormy couldn't smoothly branch out into other professions that were certainly less demanding than being a racehorse. Stormy thought eating was a fine singular profession, which, if taken seriously, could be very rigorous and time-consuming.

From Stormy's point of view, it was a medal of honor, lugging a bulging, sagging belly around, one that sometimes caused him to be mistaken for a pregnant broodmare. He could pull it all off with such aplomb. It particularly took diligent work to maintain such a curvaceous figure when he was low horse on the equine totem pole, having to learn to worm his way in to the hay pile alongside the boss horses, convincing them he was harmless while he stuffed as much hay down his throat as fast as possible.

My horse's forced entrepreneurial work with the Forest Service pack string was not on his agenda. Nor was being a wrangler's horse on the Hunewill Guest Ranch his idea, though he *did* flirt with and blink his big brown eyes at the girl wranglers, who fought over getting to ride him. (I *witnessed* the scoundrel flirting, and the girls told me he was their favorite!)

For a number of years post-racing, Stormy spent his summers in the Sierra Nevada foothills of California with the Forest Service pack string or on the dude ranch. With the eight-horse herd of the Forest Service, and the one hundred fifty-plus horse herd on the dude ranch, Stormy learned how to be a horse again: how to live on a vast acreage (forty-five hundred acres), and to learn to integrate into a very complex social totem pole. There were a couple of disasters with barbed wire fences, where he likely didn't get out of the way of some dominant horses. One of those accidents landed him in a vet clinic for eight days, followed by a month at a friend's rehab barn. He's got a white front leg scar commemorating that event. Barbed wire is the bane and boon of the West—something you just have to deal with if you choose to keep your horse on a ranch in cowboy country. I traded the risk of barbed wire accidents with the freedom of having my horse live like a horse out in the open. I think he's a better and happier horse for it.

Winters meant semi-vacation time, hanging out with endurance horses in the southern California desert. There he learned to respect some fine and somewhat famous Arabian endurance horses like Zayante and Raffiq, and he picked up their habits of cavorting around with his tail cocked in the air, as Arabians tend to do.

After Stormy followed me to Idaho, his extramural duties branched out even further in the service horse sector. He became the Owyhee Bookmobile (delivering good books to next-door neighbors), Owyhee Building Inspector (checking on the progress of a neighbor's buildings), Owyhee Official Greeter (saying hello to anybody who might have treats in their pockets, especially unwary strangers), and Owyhee Mailman (dropping letters off at the neighbor's). He often helped out as a trail marker for endurance rides, and a ribbon puller after the rides. He walked the dogs.

He was calm enough (read: lazy) to give my seventeen-year-old niece Amanda her first-ever ride on a horse, and he was challenging enough (read: lazy) to give ten-year-old Sarah some good riding lessons on a harder-to-control (read: lazy) horse.

His favorite chore has always been Resident Lawnmower; but there was the day he was recruited to be a Babysitter. It turned out completely different from how any of us expected.

When a new horse arrives on your farm, you don't just throw him in with the already-close-knit big herd, unless you're looking to get him mercilessly chased around, and likely injured. And in the West, you always have barbed wire fences to deal with, and not all horses know the danger of barbed wire and that they best stay out of it. Best option is to pen the newcomer up with one other horse, with plenty of room for him to maneuver himself out of tight situations, so he can sniff the rest of the herd over a sturdy fence for a few days until they all get partially acquainted, before turning him loose with everybody.

We thought Stormy was the perfect candidate to babysit the new arrival, four-year-old Tex (from Texas of course), for a few days while the rest of the herd introductions were made over the fence. As one of the lowest ranking, but mellow, and well tolerated, horses in the Owyhee herd, Stormy could provide both companionship and a fairly non-threatening introduction to the new resident.

Being permanently ensconced near the bottom of the herd totem pole, Stormy was always thrilled when a new baby joined the herd. Then he got to be the boss of the baby for a couple of years . . .

until the baby got wise to him and turned the big kahuna tables on him.

The big Thoroughbred towered over the Arabian Tex physically (by about six inches) and mentally (by a mile). Stormy was delighted with this new assignment of herd boss over this new little runt. He bullied Tex around with the ferocity of a wild stallion challenging an interloper, territorially guarding his hayrack, and jealously guarding his human (me).

At first.

Stormy ruled one whole day with complete supremacy over Tex. He'd charge Tex with pinned ears and bared teeth, to keep him away from his hay and human: *Back off you little punk-ass!*

Tex, not exactly *scared*, but more like *respectful* of his elder, would back quickly away from Stormy: *Yes sir, right away, sir. I'm sorry, noble sir.* Tex was quite the polite southerner.

By the second day, the picture began to change a bit. Stormy now took just a couple of semi-aggressive steps toward Tex with pinned ears and bared teeth: *Back away you little punk!*

Tex, already getting wise to his elder, would take one step back: *Um, well, OK, sir . . . I like you, sir . . .* then he'd step *toward* Stormy, forcing *him* to retreat a step. *Move over please, sir.*

By the third day, Tex pinned his ears and tossed his head up at Stormy to move him over at the hayrack, and he looked up and stared Stormy in the eyeballs: *Excuse me, sir, please scoot over, and P.S. I like you a lot.*

Stormy, with pinned ears, scurried over: *OK, you little horse, I give.*

From then on, Tex bossed his elder around politely and with obvious affection, following him everywhere around the pen, eating hay right by his side, drinking from the water trough by his side, bonding right up with his new pal, Big Brother Stormy. If Stormy dared to pin his ears to test the boss waters again, Tex completely ignored his gesture, and sidled a little closer.

They've been inseparable BFFs—Best Friends Forever—ever since. A neighbor, Linda, now owns Tex, but she boards him here. Twice she's tried to take him home and keep him at her place, and both times Tex either jumped or crawled under his fence, and he trotted himself right back up the road to our place, to be at his pal Stormy's side where he was obviously meant to be.

Stormy was Tex's first escort riding out on the Owyhee trails, exuding confidence and casualness (read: laziness) for his young, inexperienced *compadre* to imitate. Tex since went on to become a fine endurance horse, while Stormy continued to devote his concentration to lawn mowing; but the Bromance continues to this day, Tex always choosing to hang out near his best pal, eating, snoozing, or running down the canyon beside him.

While Stormy sometimes acts irritated with his shadow, anyone can tell he is secretly pleased to have the devoted attention of such an imperturbable little sidekick. Tex had no problem integrating with the rest of the herd near the top of the horse pecking order despite his size; and this has elevated Stormy's status just a little more, though all Stormy really wants to do anyway is just eat, which he does beside his little pal.

I've never galloped fast on my ex-racehorse. Oddly, after all those early racehorse-galloping dreams that shaped the direction of my horse life, it's never been anything I've been dying to do. Racing was in Stormy's past, in our past, and that's where it should stay. I don't even ride him much anymore, because he's got navicular syndrome, which leaves his front feet sore at times, and riding is not something he's particularly thrilled with anyway.

When Stormy does take me out on a short couple of rides a year, we mostly walk, a couple of miles up the canyon and back. He'll let me know if he thinks it's too much for him, because when I nudge him forward, he'll grunt with feigned exertion. He grunted a lot when the ten-year-old rode him in lessons.

Fall and winter are my two favorite seasons of the year to ride Stormy, and I like to think he enjoys the golden autumn leaves and the crisp, cool air. He used to freak out when he found himself a couple of miles out on a trail by himself, but as long as we don't go too far, he seems to get into it once we're out there, and agree with me that the Owyhee country is not a bad place to be astride a horse. When Stormy's sound, we do some trotting, and he's a smooth and powerful mover. I feel big and important on my sixteen-hand Thoroughbred, who once took on and conquered the world (or a small part of it), on the racetrack.

Never would I admit that my horse is spoiled, but Stormy's sure got my number. When he comes up to the barn, all he has to do is give me *that special look,* and I automatically fetch him a treat from the tack room. When I feed grain to some of the other working endurance horses, all Stormy has to do is give me *that special nicker,* and of course I have to fetch him a little grain, even though the last time I can recall him working hard enough to earn grain is sometime around 2002. Sometimes I'll let him out to wander the grounds on his own. He'll usually head straight for the grass so he can get to work on mowing the lawn.

I don't brush him (he has always *hated* being brushed). I never trim his mane. I'll comb out his tail if it gets a knot in it; but he lives like a wild horse now, hippie-long hair, unpolished hide, dirt and all. Dapples still spring out from his coat several times a year. He just looks healthy and happy, being a horse in a herd, with free-choice hay year-round, with his own human around to gaze at him fondly and give him head hugs and neck scratches. Sadly, not all ex-racehorses end up this way.

Despite the lack of grooming I (don't) do on him, Stormy's an accomplished model for my horse photography, even in his rugged-looking phases. His mug has appeared four times on the cover of magazines. He learned to pose well on the racetrack, where I first started shooting him all those years ago. It never goes to his head, though; he accepts the spotlight pragmatically.

It's the adoration that he gets from me that he loves best: when I grab his head and plant a kiss on his nose, when I wrap my arms around his neck and hug him. He deserves it.

I sometimes think back to those goals I had, of riding fast and wild and free on a horse. Had I achieved that long-ago dream of galloping racehorses, I never would have spent my years as a groom, and Stormy likely would never have come into my life. I never would have met, taken care of, gotten close to, and loved, Stormy.

There were many branching paths leading away from that humiliating failure of that shattered galloping dream. I blithely followed them, not knowing where they would lead. One path had led me to The Most Beautiful Horse on the Planet: Stormy, my Love.

APPENDIX NOTES

OF BITS AND PIECES

For extras–photos and videos, see the links for each chapter at www.TheEquestrianVagabond.com/Soul_Deep_In_Horses.html.

• THE COVER •

I wanted my "Tribe" to participate in my book, and not just by reading it after it was published. I asked my readers to vote on which of my horse photographs should be used as the cover shot. As a photographer, sometimes it's hard for me to judge my own photos objectively. I narrowed my choices to seven favorites (with difficulty), and threw the choices out there. By a large majority, my readers picked "Gold Dust"—the golden, dusty silhouette photo you now see on the cover. The horse is Rhett, Steph's beloved heart horse, who makes an appearance in chapter twenty.

And that "Horse Laugh" photo before the Table of Contents? That's Stormy and the world's biggest horse yawn!

• PROLOGUE •

I liken being obsessed with horses to being obsessed with mountain climbing, which I might have gotten into in my youth, had I not grown up in flat south Texas. It's hard to explain exactly what it is that drives one to reach that rugged peak in the sky, or what compels one to climb aboard a horse to get from here to there. The fun, and the mental and physical challenges, are parts of it, but the very visceral vibes you experience and the highs you experience from getting out on the trails, trump all need to try to explain it away.

• CHAPTER 1—SHATTERED •

I ran into Homer again some twenty-five years later, on the backstretch of Emerald Downs. I wondered if he remembered this momentous event in my life. I didn't ask him, since I can still easily conjure up those feelings of embarrassment and humiliation.

See Chapter 1 extras at
www.TheEquestrianVagabond.com/Soul_Deep_In_Horses.html.

• CHAPTER 2—RIDING OUT •

I am pretty sure I lived another life, or will live a next life, in Ireland. A piece of Ireland will always be a part of my soul.

See Chapter 2 extras at
www.theequestrianvagabond.com/Soul_Deep_In_Horses.html.

• CHAPTER 3—RACING IN THE RAIN •

Obviously, this was back in the days before cell phones, or internet. There were pay phones or card-phones in the streets in countries around the world.

The common tsessebe (Damaliscus lunatus) are technically not antelope. They are one of a number of species of the subfamily Alcelaphinae in the family Bovidae. To many of us species-challenged humans, we erroneously refer to Tsessebe generally as "antelope", just as we erroneously refer to the pronghorn (Antilocapra americana—family Antilocapridae) around here in Owyhee County, Idaho, as "antelope", which, technically, they are not.

I am not sure why I wasn't afraid to gallop on this unfamiliar horse in a foreign country. I can only attribute it to being a Traveler. I'm a different person when I travel—less constrained, thinking less "in a box". More things are simply possible when you travel. I didn't wear a helmet that day. I never ride without one now.

See Chapter 3 extras at
www.theequestrianvagabond.com/Soul_Deep_In_Horses.html.

• CHAPTER 4–LABOR OF LOVE •

This story was originally published in *The Texas Thoroughbred* magazine, and it won both first place Personal Column, and the Merial Human-Animal Bond Award in the 2004 American Horse Publications Awards.

This chapter is a shout-out for grooms in the racing industry. The trainers and jockeys always get the glory. Occasionally an exercise rider's name is mentioned, if they regularly ride for a stable where he or she gallops a famous horse or two. Rarely will you ever hear mention of the grooms, who do spend the most time with the racehorses they care for.

"Gg3/4" is interpreted as "Gallop (work) from the gate 3/4 mile". A routine gallop would be simply "G", and often the exercise rider who knows the horse well will know the best exercise for the horse, say a two-minute lick once around the track (faster than a gallop but not a full-on work), or perhaps a two-mile jog backtracking on the outside rail (against the galloping traffic). A "W" would be a day off, or a "Walk" for the horse where he simply spends thirty to sixty minutes walking in circles on the walker. Of course all trainers have their own shorthand for their charts, and all barns and trainers and horses have their own routines.

Lasix is a diuretic drug given to "bleeders"—horses who have been shown, by endoscopic exam, to bleed from the lungs during or after a race. "Bleeding" is another term for EIPH, or exercise induced pulmonary hemorrhage. Generally, the higher the speed, the more incidence of EIPH (it is rare, for example, in endurance horses, who don't run full out). One study showed 80% of racehorses having evidence of hemorrhage. Lasix is used as a preventative for EIPH, though it has not been proven that it is a cure. However, there are some handicappers who believe a horse will run well his first time on Lasix, which is why you'll see a "1L" in a racing form, meaning a horse is running his first time on Lasix. The therapeutic use of Lasix is a continuing controversy in Thoroughbred racing—some people say all drugs should be eliminated from racing, while some argue

Lasix is necessary and beneficial for horses that bleed into their lungs, when racing full out. Medication rules vary from state to state.

See Chapter 4 extras at
www.theequestrianvagabond.com/Soul_Deep_In_Horses.html.

• CHAPTER 5—THE ROMANCE WAS GONE •

It was terribly sad to see Longacres racetrack die, after sixty years of operation (1933-1992). The Boeing Company bought it, bulldozed it, and built an office park over the site in Renton, Washington.

Many non-profit organizations took up the cause of the plight of "used up" racehorses, organizing rescues, buying Thoroughbreds out of the slaughter pens, providing care for them till their lives ended naturally. I'm a member of The Exceller Fund (see www.ExcellerFund.org), which was formed in 1997, three months after the Hall of Fame racehorse Exceller died in a slaughterhouse at age twenty-three in Sweden because his owner thought he no longer had a value as a breeding stallion. In the last decade, the Thoroughbred racing industry has stepped up to the plate, acknowledging the need for care of Thoroughbreds after their racing careers are over, and contributing to some of these organizations. Much must still be done, but it's a start.

Emerald Downs was built in Auburn, about ten miles from the Longacres site. It opened in 1996. Emerald Downs still holds the world records for two distances: 1:00.87 for 5 1/2 furlongs, set on April 22, 2012, by 5-year-old Hollywood Harbor; and 1:13 for 6 1/2 furlongs, set on May 22, 2005, by 7-year-old Sabertooth.

Stormy never ran as short as 5 1/2 furlongs; and the closest Stormy ever finished at 6 1/2 furlongs was a fourth place. All of his wins were at 6 furlongs.

I tracked Joey down several years after I left the track. He was owned by some guy who rode him and used him as an occasional packhorse. Joey seemed happy and well taken care of. I lost touch with him after that, and felt quite guilty about it.

See Chapter 5 extras at
www.theequestrianvagabond.com/Soul_Deep_In_Horses.html.

From the www.AERC.org website:

"The American Endurance Ride Conference (AERC) was founded in 1972 as a national governing body for long distance riding. Over the years it has developed a set of rules and guidelines designed to provide a standardized format and strict veterinary controls. At the same time it has sought to avoid the rigidity and complexity so characteristic of many other equine disciplines.

"In addition to promoting the sport of endurance riding, the AERC encourages the use, protection, and development of equestrian trails, especially those with historic significance. Many special events of four to six consecutive days take place over historic trails, such as the Pony Express Trail, the Outlaw Trail, the Chief Joseph Trail, and the Lewis and Clark Trail. The founding ride of endurance riding, the Western States Trail Ride or "Tevis," covers 100 miles of the famous Western States and Immigrant Trails over the Sierra Nevada Mountains. These rides promote awareness of the importance of trail preservation for future generations and foster an appreciation of our American heritage.

"AERC Mission Statement: To promote the sport of endurance riding and to encourage and enforce the safe use of horses in demonstrating their endurance abilities in a natural setting through the development, use and preservation of trails. Further, AERC's mission is to maintain horse and ride records of event competition and completions, to record and provide awards to outstanding horses and riders, to ensure that all sanctioned events are conducted in a safe, fair and consistent manner, and to actively promote and conduct educational efforts and research projects that will foster a high level of safety and enjoyment for all horses and riders. The above is to be accomplished with the understanding that goals for the rider must be meshed with the abilities of the horse. Part of AERC's mission is to attract and reward members who act to insure the highest priority for their horses' immediate and long-term physical and emotional health and well-being."

Contact AERC to join, or to start learning about getting yourself addicted to endurance riding!

Julie Suhr's autobiography, *Ten Feet Tall, Still: The Very Personal 70-Year Odyssey Of A Woman Who Still Pursues Her Childhood Passion*, is one of my Top Twenty books, ever. You can find it on Amazon.com. She's also author of . . . *but it wasn't the horse's fault! a rambling catchall,* available at www.marinerapublishing.com.

See Chapter 6 extras at www.theequestrianvagabond.com/Soul_Deep_In_Horses.html.

• CHAPTER 7—THE VISIT •

During Stormy's last year on the racetrack (the year I didn't take care of him), he had eleven starts with one win, and the rest unplaced, with total earnings of $4,155. He started out the year running for a $16,000 claiming tag, then jumped to $20,000 in his next race, where he lost his rider, then steadily dropped in class until he hit the bottom, $3,200 claiming. He won that race, in which Chris happened to claim him. Stormy started three times for Chris, with a fifth place being his best finish, before she took him home for the winter, at which time I had my fateful reunion with him.

Stormy and I made a video showing off his wicked tongue scar!

See Chapter 7 extras at www.theequestrianvagabond.com/Soul_Deep_In_Horses.html.

• CHAPTER 8—ROCKY START •

Vet checks are part of every AERC endurance ride. There are one or two (or more) vet checks in every 25-mile and 50-mile ride, and three or more in every 75-mile or 100-mile ride. Every horse must be inspected by a veterinarian, and get a passing grade on his heart rate (which usually must be sixty beats per minute), muscle tone, hydration, and gait; he must be declared "fit to continue" on to the next vet check. At the end of the ride, the horse has thirty or sixty minutes to come down to the pulse criteria, and pass all the parameters, and be declared "fit to continue" to get a completion for the ride.

Riders carry vet cards with them that the veterinarians mark at each vet check, to keep track of the horses' well-being.

The vet checks usually have a hold of thirty minutes to an hour so the horses can eat and rest.

Ribbons are usually used to mark trails; sometimes ride managers use spray-painted arrows on the ground, or white flour along the trails to mark the direction to go. If you live in areas where your trails go through cow country, you'll know that cows tend to eat bright colored ribbons, so you hope you have trees where you can hang the ribbons high enough where the cows can't reach them. I have been known to spray-paint cow patties, because the cows don't eat their own poo!

At night, glowsticks are usually hung for the riders to follow. It can be pitch black, but horses can see in the dark where we humans can't. Sometimes, you just have to trust your horse to stay on trail!

A good number of endurance horses have moved from shoes to "barefoot", with hoof protection used during rides. There are various types of hoof boots used on the barefoot horses, the most common of which are Easyboot and Renegade, both of which are technologically advancing every year.

I don't canter down hills anymore! One has to have a very sure-footed, balanced horse, or else be fearless, or have no clue, to canter down hills. I ride some very sure-footed, balanced horses, but I still don't canter down hills on purpose!

See Chapter 8 extras at
www.theequestrianvagabond.com/Soul_Deep_In_Horses.html.

• CHAPTER 9—THE MOST BEAUTIFUL HORSE ON THE PLANET •

I visited Chris on the backstretch of Emerald Downs twelve years after I got Stormy from her. She became a top trainer there.

See Chapter 9 extras at
www.theequestrianvagabond.com/Soul_Deep_In_Horses.html.

• CHAPTER 10—CRASH •

Zak was mostly blind in his right eye—but I am certain it had no bearing on his accident.

I went to visit the Forest Service horses a couple of years after my FS career. Sadly, I eventually lost touch with them. I'm afraid to call and find out what happened to them.

Margaret gave one of the old Forest Service horses, Woody, a Forever Home.

Stormy and Woody lived together for a while over a winter in Ridgecrest, California. They opened their Christmas presents together that year!

See Chapter 10 extras at
www.theequestrianvagabond.com/Soul_Deep_In_Horses.html.

• CHAPTER 11–SHATTERED II •

While I forget the names of my awesome surgeons, they get another Thank You, as well as John Petersmith Hospital in Fort Worth, which I highly recommend if you shatter your face and need to have it put back together.

You won't see online extras from this chapter, so page onward!

• CHAPTER 12–THE WORLD'S GREATEST HORSEMAN •

Zayante was named to the AERC Hall of Fame in 2002.

Jackie Bumgardner and her other good horse (and Zayante's best friend) Ross, a.k.a. Sierra Fadrazal+/, won the AERC Pard'ners Award in 1998.

You can read more about the great Zayante on my blog page under "The Rainbow Bridge".

See Chapter 12 extras at
www.theequestrianvagabond.com/Soul_Deep_In_Horses.html.

• CHAPTER 13–HONEY IN THE DESERT •

Egyptian history is fascinating. If you ever want a good lesson, particularly on horseback, go see Maryanne! She keeps an entertaining and fascinating Cairo/Giza Daily Photo blog, at:

http://cairogizadailyphoto.blogspot.com.

The Western Desert (also known as the Libyan Desert) is the northern and eastern part of the Sahara Desert, which Maryanne will tell you, technically means "Desert Desert", since "Sahara" in Arabic means "desert".

The Great Pyramid of Giza is part of the Giza Necropolis, which includes several pyramid complexes, mastabas (tombs), and the Great Sphinx. The Great Pyramid (the largest one, known as the Pyramid of Cheops or Khufu) is one of the Seven Wonders of the Ancient World. *The Complete Pyramids: Solving the Ancient Mysteries* by Mark Lehner is an excellent book on many of the major pyramids of Ancient Egypt, if you can't get your own history lessons from Maryanne.

The "Melted Pyramid" is a local name for the Black Pyramid, or the Pyramid of Amenemhat III, in the Dashur area. It's very eroded, caving in upon itself, with a very awesome, imposing presence despite its decay.

The Bent Pyramid is also part of the Dashur complex, built by the Pharaoh Sneferu. The lower part of the pyramid's angle is steeper; it is said that during construction, to continue building at this angle, the pyramid would have been so tall and steep it would have been unstable, so the angle of the upper part of the pyramid was eased. The result looks like a "bent" pyramid.

The Red Pyramid, also known as the North Pyramid, is also part of the Dashur necropolis. It is so named for the reddish shade of its granite stones. Pharaoh Sneferu also built this one.

We rode into the desert near what we called "the Sun Temple", but according to the Abu Sir Papyri—archives of Old Kingdom documents written in hieratic and found in one of the Abu Sir pyramids—there are *six* Sun Temples. Only two have been discovered. This one we rode by was formally known as King Niuserre's "Delight of Re". Both were built during the Fifth Dynasty and were dedicated to the worship of Re (or Ra), the ancient Egyptian Sun-God. The area of this sun temple is Abu Ghorab, which means, much to the Delight of Merri, "Father of Crows".

A "wadi" is a gully between hills.

"Japanese Hill" is so-called by the locals because of the Japanese excavation of the Abu Sir complex. "The Egyptology name of the hill is Lion Hill," Maryanne says, "because it looks like a sleeping lion when you approach it from the southeast." The site contains pre-pharaonic, pharaonic, and Greco-Roman antiquities, so it's a special area.

See Chapter 13 extras at www.theequestrianvagabond.com/Soul_Deep_In_Horses.html.

• CHAPTER 14—PARADE FEVER •

Stormy didn't participate with the Forest Service horses in the parade, since by this time he was living and working on the Hunewill Guest Ranch in the summers. The Hunewill Guest Ranch offers authentic western ranch vacations in the summers. The ranch was founded in 1861 as a working cattle ranch; the Guest Ranch part of it started in the 1930's. They don't normally take on boarders, but they were kind enough not only to board Stormy for me in the summers, but also to put him to work!

See Chapter 14 extras at www.theequestrianvagabond.com/Soul_Deep_In_Horses.html.

• CHAPTER 15—MY KING •

There are many different interpretive English spellings of the Egyptian galabiya. I chose this one. And anyway, the plural of galabiya is, properly, "galaleeb".

Fellahin are Egyptian peasants or farmers.

Gamoosas are water buffalo. And the proper plural is "gawamees".

The canals in the Egyptian countryside are one thing that gave me the Willies. They ultimately carried water from the Nile (water you don't want to touch anyway), and by the time they got to the countryside, they contained a lot of extras: garbage, animal and human waste, floating *things*, submerged *things*, and more *things*. I once saw a dead pig in a canal, and I expect that was one of the more benign floating *things*. I am sure the canals contain parasites and organisms that have yet to be classified by science.

On my return to Egypt a year later, I still thought of Harry. I asked what happened to him, but all I learned was "He went to another stable." I hoped and dreamed he had a good life, because some of those Pyramid stables were dreadful affairs if you were a four-legged creature.

Egyptians do seem to have a lot of stallions rather than geldings. Of course, there are a lot of nice bloodlines in Egypt; but on the other hand, many stallions make nice geldings. I once asked Morad about this Stallion Thing, and why didn't the Egyptians geld more of their stallions; and he took it personally, protectively shrinking and covering himself and turning a squeamish color.

See Chapter 15 extras at
www.theequestrianvagabond.com/Soul_Deep_In_Horses.html.

• CHAPTER 16—MY ROCKET SHIP •

The Akhal-teke is a breed that originated in Turkmenistan. They are often lean and streamlined (think: greyhound in dogs), and are known for their speed and endurance.

See Chapter 16 extras at
www.theequestrianvagabond.com/Soul_Deep_In_Horses.html.

• CHAPTER 17—THE LAST RIDE •

Zayante's colic episode was mysterious—no obvious cause such as a gut twist or obstruction. It was a random event that could have happened to him out at pasture. (I discovered Stormy randomly colicking out in his pasture one day—he got better with a dose of banamine, though it made me wonder how many times we don't even *see* our horses colic, if we aren't monitoring them twenty-four hours a day.) Zay retired and lived out his years with his best pal Ross; and after Ross died, Zayante lived with Nick and Judy. He died of colic on November 5, 2013, and is still mourned by all of us who knew and loved him.

He is listed with 13,200 AERC miles on one list, 13,250 on another. Either way, as of 2013 he's still sixth on the all-time list of high-mileage endurance equines.

See Chapter 17 extras at
www.theequestrianvagabond.com/Soul_Deep_In_Horses.html.

• CHAPTER 18—RIDERS OF ROHAN •

Trevor did indeed break in a colt in a couple of hours. I even helped by getting on the colt. I would not have believed it if I hadn't witnessed it. I recorded the event in my blog.

See Chapter 18 extras at
www.theequestrianvagabond.com/Soul_Deep_In_Horses.html.

• CHAPTER 19—BEACHIN' IT •

Horses are measured in "hands"—four inches to a hand. The measurement goes from the top of the withers to the ground. A sixteen-hand horse is five feet, four inches at the withers. That's a fairly large horse to climb aboard . . . i.e. it's a long way to the ground from his back!

An Anglo-Arabian is half Arabian, half Thoroughbred. Fritz got his size from his Thoroughbred lines.

See Chapter 19 extras at
www.theequestrianvagabond.com/Soul_Deep_In_Horses.html.

• CHAPTER 20—WANNA BE A COWGIRL •

When you live up the crick in Idaho, you tend to call it "crick" instead of "creek".

It might look easy rounding up cattle. Cows and calves aren't so difficult, but I don't mess around with bulls anymore. They are too big and powerful and unpredictable—one or two thousand pounds of pure unbendable steel. Bulls tend to take offense at everything that interferes with their personal agenda. They'll go right through a barbed wire fence, or anything else in their way. I watched one bull stick his head underneath a cowboy's horse and lift him right up in the air. Fortunately the bull had no horns, and the horse didn't panic, and the cowboy stayed on. But that's not any ride I want to experience!

I recorded a couple of those rough bull round-ups I was glad not to be a part of in my blog.

Rhett left us to cross the Rainbow Bridge in January of 2014. If there is a Horse God, there will be no cows in Horse Heaven (surely that is the name of a Country Western song somewhere!). Rhett is on the cover of this book, silhouetted in golden sunlight on a very dusty Owyhee day.

See Chapter 20 extras at
www.theequestrianvagabond.com/Soul_Deep_In_Horses.html.

• CHAPTER 21–JE SUIS PERDU •

Bridle paths, or bridleways, often developed in Europe in historic times as transport routes for horses, where the terrain was too difficult for wagons to drive. In some countries they still exist as the main route between villages, but most often they are used for recreation.

Really, I am comically terrible at pronouncing French words. My French-speaking Belgian friends get a great kick out of listening to me try.

See Chapter 21 extras at
www.theequestrianvagabond.com/Soul_Deep_In_Horses.html.

• CHAPTER 22–MY KINDRED SPIRIT •

John and Steph Teeter of Idaho started the website www.Endurance.net in 1994. It was John T's brainchild, and it was among the first 1000 websites in existence. It grew into the world's leading website for covering endurance riding events around the world. Steph traveled around the world for endurance, and she really is friends with an endurance-riding king! I began working for Endurance.net in 2007 as a photographing, writing, traveling rider.

Steph also created AERC's first website in the mid-1990's.

A sidepull is a type of bit-less bridle. It's a sort of variation of a hackamore, but with less mechanical action. You won't have much pull on a horse that runs off if he's only wearing a sidepull, so you better trust your horse!

I made a video of Jose giving himself a bath with the water hose I'm holding.

You thought I made up the story of Jose holding up a bucket to Kazam after biting him on the butt, didn't you—it's in my blog.

See Chapter 22 extras at
www.theequestrianvagabond.com/Soul_Deep_In_Horses.html.

• CHAPTER 23—MY LOVE •

Stormy ran from age three through age seven, with a lifetime total of forty-two starts, six wins, nine seconds, and four thirds.

Stormy has (so far!) been on the cover of four magazines.

See Chapter 23 extras at
www.theequestrianvagabond.com/Soul_Deep_In_Horses.html.

ABOUT THE AUTHOR

Merri Melde, a.k.a. The Equestrian Vagabond, is a horse photographer, writer, author, photojournalist, artist, horse packer, carriage driver, racetrack groom, spotted owl hooter, wildlife technician, Raven fanatic, trail builder, sound engineer, theatre techie, world traveler, owner of The Most Beautiful Horse On The Planet (Stormy), rabid obsessed endurance rider, and Tevis Cup finisher. But not all at the same time.

Merri has written for over a dozen magazines, and photographed for over two dozen magazines around the world, and traveled in over three dozen countries, sometimes seeking adventure and enlightenment, and often chasing horses.

She's the author of the short stories, *Traveler Tales,* and *Racehorse Tales,* available on Amazon.com.

Visit www.TheEquestrianVagabond.com to contact Merri and see her published works.

ACKNOWLEDGMENTS

Writing a memoir is rather a life-long journey, from the beginning of the adventures long ago (in my case, at birth), to the final punching of the "publish" button. For the entire jaunt, my family has been along for the rides, the good rides and the bad ones, but they never discouraged me. They might have been concerned or aghast at times, but by and large I think they've mostly enjoyed the adventures. They've been particularly encouraging and helpful in my entire book writing and publishing process. In fact I followed my big brother's footsteps in publishing a book! (See *Summit Views: The Lure of the Mountains* by John Melde on Amazon.com.) It really has been a fun family affair, and I thank them with all my heart. (Stormy does too!)

I am inexpressibly indebted to my super beta and proofreaders and editors, SherpaMatty, Jean Barney, Aarene Storms (author of *Endurance 101),* and Elizabeth Funderburk.

Pat Barnhardt (www.writingdownpat.net) was my Editor with a capital E; and aside from being very patient with me, she did a wonderful job. She tolerated my creative words and unusual tense choices, among other things! Thank you to author extraordinaire Milton C. Toby, and to managing editor/senior editor/proofreader extraordinaire Bobbie Jo Lieberman for the blurbs and the encouragement. Thank you, Julie Suhr—friend, icon, author, mentor.

Thank you to all my horse friends who had horses that "needed rode" over the years (or, dare I say decades), and to all of them who shared my adventures.

Thank you to my fans of The Equestrian Vagabond blog, who also encouraged me to get my book written already, after I'd mildly threatened to do so for quite some time.

And, of course thanks to all the wonderful horses, who got me to where I am today, one way or another, by teaching me to always remember to listen to, and learn from them.

THANK YOU!

Thank you for reading *Soul Deep in Horses: Memoir of an Equestrian Vagabond!* I hope you enjoyed riding along with me on this memoir of my horse life, and getting to know some of my best four-legged equine friends. The stories don't end here, of course. The horses always present some new and unexpected adventures, which beg telling. There are more to come!

As a writer, I love hearing your comments on my stories. You can write me at authortheequestrianvagabond@gmail.com, and tell me what you loved and didn't love; and please visit my web page at www.TheEquestrianVagabond.com.

Your voice is important! If you enjoyed this book, please pass the word. I would also be grateful if you'd take the time to leave a short review on my Amazon author page, where you'll find all my books and short stories: http://amzn.to/1hI80ie.

If you'd like to be the first to know of my next writing projects and entertaining brouhahas, sign up for my newsletter, The Equestrian Vagabond Dispatch, at http://www.theequestrianvagabond.com/Soul_Deep_In_Horses_News.html.

Happy trails!

Merri Melde
The Equestrian Vagabond

Made in the USA
Charleston, SC
10 November 2015